awakening grace

spiritual practices to transform your soul

Matt LeRoy

Jeremy Summers

wesleyan
publishing
house

Indianapolis, Indiana

Copyright © 2012 by Matt LeRoy and Jeremy Summers
Published by Wesleyan Publishing House
Indianapolis, Indiana 46250
Printed in the United States of America
ISBN: 978-0-89827-431-8

Library of Congress Cataloging-in-Publication Data

LeRoy, Matthew.
    Awakening grace : spiritual practices to transform your soul /
Matt LeRoy, Jeremy Summers.
        p. cm.
    Includes bibliographical references (p.).
    ISBN 978-0-89827-431-8
    1. Spiritual life--Christianity. 2. Christian life. 3. Spiritual formation.
I. Summers, Jeremy. II. Title.
    BV4501.3.L47 2012
    248.4'6--dc23
                                                2011047916

To the memory of Mary Ann Presher. A beautiful life, fully awake to grace. And to Sarah, Luke, and Samuel. Signs and symbols of God's faithful love.

—Matt LeRoy

To Andrea, my best friend and precious bride, you teach me how to love and live in grace. And to our children, Macy, Ava, Micah, and Ty, you remind me daily of what it means to be a child of God.

—Jeremy Summers

contents

foreword

My grandfather was a sawyer from the mountains of West Virginia. He was a man of few words, and when he lived with us the last few years of his life, my brothers and I learned that every word he spoke was deemed, at least to his mind, worthy of breaking the precious silence he privileged. One day I found him in our basement, working on a door.

"Watcha' doin', Grandpa?" Without looking up, he pulled out a handkerchief, blew his nose, and said, "Son, there's three kind of broken things in this world. There's the kind which, when they are broke, will fix themselves if we leave them alone. A lot of things in life are like that, more than we realize. Then there's the kind of broke things that only God can fix. And then, Lenny, there's the kind which, when they are broke, I got to fix. That's what I'm doin' now—fixin' this door!"

There's a lot of "fixin" going on in the church today. Almost every book is a "fixer upper" in some way. Some are trying to fix things that will fix themselves over time if we are patient. Others are trying to fix things that only God can fix, solutions which can only be accomplished by prayer (Mark 9). Once in a while there comes along that rare resource that recognizes which is which, and writes accordingly.

You have in your hands one of those special gifts. This little book has it all. It's the Swiss army knife of church revitalization books. It comes with the knife of deep theology, a poker-probe of church history, a screw that uncorks Bible study, a spoonful of spiritual apps, and study-guide scissors at the end of each chapter. Most importantly, its USB stick (the new knives have gone digital) reframes the whole discussion of "spiritual disciplines" away from Latinate routines and toward living litanies that are based on daily participation in God's mission in the world.

The word *participation* is key. It's what turns a belief into faith or a sign into a symbol. I learned this from the French philosopher, Pascal expert, and theologian Émile Cailliet. Cailliet was a charter member of the board of the Princeton-based publication *Theology Today*. Cailliet's distinction between sign and symbol is as follows:

> Here is a Roman soldier, seeing the design of a fish. For him, it is a sign that Christians are 'round and about. It leaves him cold but alert. Later, a cautious Christian passes by and suddenly sees the fish. Immediately his heart pounds

and his mind is filled with rich associations. To him, this fish drawing is emphatically not a sign. It is a symbol. Clearly, what animates the symbol, makes a symbol a symbol, in the final analysis, is the sense of participation. To me, a symbol should be defined as a sign of an experienced participation.

Here is a distinction that is at the heart of the spiritual practices in *Awakening Grace*. Christian faith is based on God's symbolic participation with us through Jesus Christ. The Christian life mandates our experienced participation in and with Christ, the Lord of life.

You have in your hands, what are, to my mind, some of the best spiritual practices or experienced participations that can turn the sign of the fish into a symbol of faith and fix any life that seeks a future of growing realization of the presence and power of God.

LEONARD SWEET
E. Stanley Jones professor, Drew University
distinguished visiting professor,
George Fox University

preface

This is a book about grace. It is about the practical implications of the world's most impractical idea. It is about awakening to the ways God shapes us into the image of his Son, through the cultivating work of the Holy Spirit. It is about exploring the well-worn paths and pioneering trails of discipleship—the ancient and innovative practices of our faith. It is about responding to, walking in, and growing in grace.

acknowledgements

We would like to thank Don Cady and Kevin Scott from Wesleyan Publishing House for their belief in this book and their work throughout the process to make it better.

We are deeply grateful for the voices of wisdom that shaped this book and continue to shape us. Dallas Willard, J. D. Walt, Keith Drury, Robert Biggs, Keith Matthews, Dan LeRoy, Jim Dunn, Steve DeNeff, and Sandra Richter—through writing, teaching, mentoring, and friendship, your influence is evident in these pages.

A special thanks to Love Chapel Hill. You are a testing ground for the ideas in this book, a tangible example of what transformation looks like in the real lives of real people. Thank you for living as an experiment in grace.

And to our friends and colleagues in the Spiritual Formation Department of The Wesleyan Church. Thank you for your heart and faithfulness to the most vital work—making disciples of Jesus.

1

a foundation

from mastery to submission

Scribbled on an orange sticky note stuck to the
back cover of a well-worn Bible is this charge: "When
you open this beautiful book, aim for submission, not
mastery."[1] These words come from one of our mentors,
J. D. Walt. Though simple, they illuminate a somewhat
counterintuitive approach to spiritual formation.

We often see discipleship as the process of mastering
the spiritual disciplines. The formula follows this pattern:
If we can get a handle on these disciplines and perform
them with excellence, then we can produce the proper
and correlating fruit. But perhaps this approach is
backwards.

calling out

Aslan probably said it best. Somehow that's not
surprising, is it?

In his classic children's tale *The Silver Chair*, C. S.
Lewis wrote of two school kids and their unlikely
adventure in the magical land of Narnia. Outsiders

Eustace Scrubb and Jill Pole desperately longed to escape the burdens of their boarding school. Connected by their shared hatred of that place, Eustace trusted Jill with a wild secret—a story of another world with talking animals and enchanted kingdoms. Hoping to somehow find a way into this world, they called out the name of Aslan, the mighty Lion and King of Narnia.

By some strange magic, their hopes were heard. Soon, Jill found herself face to face with the great (and good) Lion. To her surprise, he commissioned her for an important task.

"Please, what task, Sir?" said Jill.

"The task for which I called you and him here out of your own world."

This puzzled Jill very much. "It's mistaking me for someone else," she thought. She didn't dare to tell the Lion this, though she felt things would get into a dreadful muddle unless she did.

"Speak your thought, Human Child," said the Lion.

"I was wondering—I mean—could there be some mistake? Because nobody called me and Scrubb, you know. It was we who asked to come here. Scrubb said we were to call to—to Somebody—it was a name I wouldn't know— and perhaps the Somebody would let us in. And we did, and then we found the door open."

"You would not have called to me unless I had been calling to you," said the Lion.[2]

And there it is. Deep theology disguised as a bedtime story. By way of the Lion, Lewis lets us taste the ways of God's rich grace. Before we ever recognized our need for him, his gentle strength was drawing us in. Before we even knew what name to call, he was calling ours. We could never find him if he hadn't already searched us out. Grace is good like that.

The eighteenth-century Reformer John Wesley spoke of this "prevenient grace" (or "grace that goes before") as the dawn breaking in on the human heart. It is the kind gift of God that calls out to us, so we can call out to him.

In his mercy, our Father draws us. He turns our heart toward him, enabling us to believe in his Son. Without this awakening grace, our sinful, broken hearts would remain hard as stone, refusing his free gift of full salvation.

His grace offers the gift. And his grace enables us to receive it. God's love for us awakens our love for him.

Without God's grace, our salvation is not possible. But we often miss that the same is true of the spiritual growth that happens after salvation. Just like salvation, discipleship is impossible without the same enabling mercy that first searched us out.

17

practicing the pathways

We easily fall into thinking that the work of spiritual formation rests on us. That it is our duty to master the disciplines of Bible reading, justice, prayer, and service. But these practices are not the focus. God is. These practices are pathways that lead us to him. These disciplines are not the end but the means of grace.

Christian practices are patterns of cooperative human activity in which the inner life takes shape over time in response to the Word and work of Christ. Our practices become a conversation between our actions and our beliefs, and are a balance between being and doing. However, Christian practices must not be mistaken for duties, but rather patterns of communal action that create openings in our lives where the grace, mercy, and presence of God may be made known to us. They are places where the power of God is experienced. Therefore, in the end, Christian practices are forms of participation in the work of God.

As we engage these pathways, we humbly submit to God's work in our lives. We open ourselves up to what we call awakening grace.

awakening grace

Awakening grace is the strength at work in these ancient and innovative practices that shape us into Christ's image. It is the grace that draws us into this process of spiritual formation and our guide along the journey. Alive in these practices—these means of grace—is a power that is actively shaping, forming, and creating us anew into the likeness of Jesus, whom we pursue and are captured by.

It is vital to understand that the power is not in the acts themselves and certainly not in our performance of them. The power is initiated through God's own presence in the process. It is his engagement with us that gives meaning to our practice.

a simple shift

This book proposes a simple shift in our view of spiritual formation. The shift concerns the agent of action in the growth process, placing the emphasis on God's grace at work in the practice instead of on our performance of the action. Of course, this is not a new idea, but it seems to be a lost one. This simple shift is illustrated by three mini-shifts.

from mastery of a discipline to submission to grace

As mentioned earlier, we often view the spiritual practices as disciplines that we should master. We strive to be better at prayer, reading Scripture, and worship—all of which, we conclude, will make us better Christians. While we absolutely need to engage with these practices, we must never think that we wrestle our way into Christian maturity by the sweat of our souls. Yes, we work at it. Yes, we struggle. But we always acknowledge that the agent of change in this journey is the grace of God.

19

Our invitation in discipleship is to submission. We submit to the will of the Father, to the shaping work of the Spirit, and to the pattern of Christ. We don't perfect our way to being better Christians. We submit ourselves to Christ. (If you think this amounts to a lazy Christianity, then perhaps you haven't walked the difficult trail of submission lately.) As we examine these practices in the coming chapters, resist the temptation to master them and embrace the counterintuitive invitation to surrender.

from practice as a tool for growth to practice as a teacher of the soul

Another mistake we make when approaching these spiritual practices is to view them as a tool in our hands rather than a teacher of our souls. We use them to accomplish our own purposes rather than listen to what they can teach us. We read Scripture to increase in knowledge, rather than hear from the heart of God. We pray to get what we want rather than enter into communion with the Holy Spirit. We worship to feel refueled or recharged, rather than give praise and ascribe glory to the resurrected King. In this, spiritual practices become utilities for leveraging quick growth. Instead, we should hear their invitation to sit at their feet and learn.

In this book, we view the spiritual life less like a factory and more like a farm—less industrial and more organic. These practices are not components of a spiritual assembly line. They are more like open fields and hidden trails to be explored in the cultivating company of the Father, Son, and Spirit. They do not promise faster results or shortcuts around the process. In this landscape dominated by machinery and efficiency, we are called living branches nourished by the Vine, under the watchful care of the Gardener.

from growth as certain formula to discipleship as unpredictable journey

We like formulas. They clearly spell out the specific series of steps toward a desired destination. They promise us a set end if we correctly follow the prescribed measures. Formulas are predictable. Formulas are safe. Formulas are certain.

But discipleship is not. Discipleship is an unpredictable journey that promises danger and risk. Discipleship follows Jesus into the unknown (to us, never to him) and disrupts the stagnant status quo. This life with Jesus is far more like an experiment in grace. So, as we explore these spiritual practices together, do not approach them as steps in a formula to trigger a predetermined outcome. Instead, engage them as pathways to walk with Jesus. They will twist and turn, taking you deeper into the heart of the Father and fellowship with the Son, all while the Holy Spirit implores you to take the next unsure step.

21

the framework

As you journey through this book, you'll find that each chapter challenges an active response to what you've read. After exploring each of the ancient or innovative practices through the framework questions of what, why, and how, each chapter ends with the catalytic question, "So, now what?" To assist you in the formational practices, we suggest several next steps in this section for you to explore as an individual or in the context of a larger group. Also included at the end of each chapter is a built-in study guide and collection of questions to encourage further engagement. Use the questions for your own study or to facilitate a shared journey with a small group.

the invitation

Do you feel a longing to grow closer to God? Do you want to know him more? Is there something in your soul that calls out to him? Then consider that awakening desire your invitation into the deep places of discipleship. Place yourself in his hands, and allow him to shape and form your life into one that looks like Jesus? After all, you never would have called out to him if he hadn't already been calling you.

study guide

1. How do you define grace?

2. How have you experienced grace in your life?

3. What does grace have to do with spiritual growth and discipleship? (We understand the role it plays in salvation, but what about discipleship?)

4. What does it mean to "aim for submission, not mastery" when engaging the spiritual practices?

5. Why do we refer to this as a counterintuitive approach? How does your own experience match up or disagree with this idea?

6. What is meant by the title *Awakening Grace*?

7. Why is discipleship described as an unpredictable journey and an experiment in grace?

8. What is the difference between an industrial approach and an organic approach to spiritual formation?

9. Looking ahead at the spiritual practices explored in this book, what practices are you excited to study? Why?

10. Likewise, which practices make you a little nervous? Which ones do you dread discussing? Why?

11. What do you hope to get out of this experience? How do you hope to grow? What are your expectations and reservations?

2
scripture

Stories matter.

This is why we hold our breath and thrust our hope on the little hobbit and his friend. We get lost in the creative mind and imagined world of J. R. R. Tolkien's Lord of the Rings trilogy and immerse ourselves in the impossible journey of an unlikely fellowship. We will Frodo onward in his mission as he carries the weight of Middle Earth around his neck. But why?

Why does an imaginary world have such a pull on our hearts? Why do we care what happens in myths of fairies or kings and queens? It's because we want to get caught up in something like that. It's because deep down we know that stories matter.

They remind us of where we have been, what we have done, and who we are. They inspire courage, imagination, and belief. They root us in memory. They stir us to dream. Stories matter.

Especially this one . . .

what is scripture?

The Bible is a story. It is the story of God's great love for humanity, his quest to rescue and redeem his creation. This narrative recounts God's activity in the world, stretching from the original perfection of Eden to the final victory of eternity. Strange as it seems, the author invites us to participate in it.

This is the story of the God who fell in love at first sight in the garden, proposed to his people through Abraham, and wrote his love in stone and handed it to Moses. When looking for a perfect way to communicate his love, he called his church a beloved bride and named himself the strong and worthy groom. It's no mistake that the whole story finishes with a wedding. It began with a husband and wife in perfect union with God and each other. It will end with a wedding feast at the restoration of all things.

This is the story of God on a mission of rescue. What kind of God would hear the cries of slaves and actually do something about it? This one. Moved by compassion for his people, he brought the greatest empire of the ancient world to its knees and led the captives into a future of freedom.

This is the story of a King with a humble heart. Delighting in the underdog, he took down giants with sticks and stones. He raised nations from the ruins and called sons and daughters out of once-barren wombs. In the strangest reversal of all, he set aside his crown and glory and lay down his life for the salvation of his subjects. He pursued them to hell and back to win their liberation. Every kingdom the world has ever known was built on the idea that the servant must die for the king; except this one. In this compelling tale, the King died for the servant.

This is the story of the one who pioneered a new way to live and love, sparked the most significant movement the world has ever seen, and invites us to be swept up in this epic saga of rescue and redemption.

why should we read scripture?

reading as formation

If the Bible is a story, then this should change the way we approach the reading of it. The goal of Bible reading is not to just dig out principles of truth, but to dive into the story and become a participant. Robert Mulholland speaks of this tension as informational reading versus formational reading.[1] The first is an exercise of intellectual mastery. The second is a practice of heart submission. When we open our minds, ears, and hearts to what the text wants to say and to whom the text wants us to become, God's awakening grace shapes and forms us further into Christ's likeness.

To increase in knowledge of Scripture is one sign of spiritual growth. But a sharp mind must be joined with a humble heart. The deeper we venture into the Word, the further we should be drawn into the mind of Christ and shaped into his likeness. Grow in knowledge; but also hunger for humility, a true mark of the holy life.

Here is the new mantra for experiencing Scripture: Aim for submission, not mastery. The Word is not a tool (or worse yet, a weapon) in your hand. Instead, you are in the Word's hands. You are not the master. You are the student.

reading as meditation

One way to actively submit to God's work through the Word is to engage in the ancient Christian practice of meditation or contemplation. At first, these terms might seem too mystical for us. It sounds like something we should leave for old monks and nuns to get into. But meditation and contemplation are actually very common pathways open to all believers. They are simply ways to listen for God's voice to speak through his Word. It is a step beyond passive reading. It is active engagement.

In his classic work *Celebration of Discipline*, Richard Foster challenges us to rediscover the practice of meditation and contemplation. "If we hope to move beyond the superficialities of our culture, including our religious culture, we must be willing to go down into the recreating silences, into the inner world of contemplation. In their writings all the masters of meditation beckon us to be pioneers in this frontier of the Spirit."[2]

27

Meditation calls for stillness, but it also sparks movement. It demands reflection, but also active obedience. Meditation on God's Word is not about sitting in a corner somewhere surrounded by incense and candles. It is about walking with the Word through the day, letting it guide and instruct you, convict or encourage you. It is about letting Scripture run through your mind until it sinks into your heart and escapes into the world through the small, common acts of your life.

Dietrich Bonhoeffer said it this way: "In meditation God's Word seeks to enter in and remain with us. It strives to stir us, to work and operate in us, so that we shall not get away from it the whole day long. Then it will do its work in us, often without our being conscious of it."[3]

This humble practice of listening intentionally for God to speak through his Word awakens something in our souls. It calls out the courage to obey. It cultivates a desire for the deep hunger for the Bread of Life.

reading as inspiration

We hold firmly that the Scriptures are the inspired Word of God. But what do we mean by that? We mean that God himself, through the Holy Spirit, inspired human writers to record his great story of love and redemption—the account of his divine activity in the world. From the sprawling narratives to the intricate laws, gripping poetry, and timeless wisdom, the Spirit of God was active in the crafting and composing of this book. He chose specific people in specific places at specific times to record his special revelation for the world.

But we also realize that inspiration happens on two planes. As Robert Mulholland points out in his book *Shaped by the Word*, the Spirit has not given up on the work of inspiration. God inspired the writers then, but he also inspires the readers now.[4]

As we open the Word, and open ourselves, the same Spirit who inspired the poets and prophets of old enables us now to understand what we are reading. In fact, as we submissively read the text, the text also has a way of reading us, with the Spirit bringing to light areas in our lives that call for further growth and deeper surrender.

how should we read scripture?

reading the Bible in context

When approaching the sacred Word of God, we have to be careful to read it responsibly and understand it in the intended context.

in the context of the surrounding passage. We should not reduce the words of Jesus and the teachings of Scripture to simple fortune cookie sound bites or clever quotes. To lift them out of their context is to lose valuable meaning and strip away important clues to our understanding. When reading a passage of Scripture, we must orient ourselves to the surrounding passages. What comes before? What follows next?

Where does this story happen? What people groups are involved? How does this fit in the larger picture of this chapter or book?

in the context of the whole of scripture. The Word of God is a complete and coherent story of his engagement with the world. Each book and chapter is intimately linked to those that come before and behind. The separate pieces interact with and comment on one another. For instance, the teachings and actions of Jesus in the Gospels are profound and powerful when read as stand-alone stories. But read them through the lens of the Old Testament prophets, and suddenly new layers of meaning take shape in a breathtaking way. Each section of the Bible must be understood in light of the whole.

in the context of culture. While inspired by the eternal Spirit of God, specific people wrote the Bible in the context of specific times and cultures. The structures of these cultures can be seen in the pages of Scripture. We must read with these cultural contexts in mind. Take John 4, for example. In this story, Jesus asks a Samaritan woman for a drink from the well. Without understanding the time and culture of Jesus, we miss the massive meaning behind this small act. But knowing the history of hatred between the Jews and Samaritans, we are moved that Jesus would cross barriers of religion, region, and race to reach her.

in the context of our lives. The Bible is an ancient text that must be understood in that setting. But we cannot forget that it has the unquestionable power to speak directly to our lives today. While penned at a certain time, it is timeless and timely truth. It is more than an epic work of priceless literature to be studied in a detached, intellectual way. It calls for engagement. It invites us into the story. It sparks obedience born out of a personal encounter with holy love.

in the context of community. We often think of the practice of reading Scripture as a personal discipline. This is only part of the idea. Originally, the Word was read aloud in public gatherings. The practice of hearing and doing was a shared act within the context of a larger community. The Spirit calls us to this same, shared experience today. Just as this sacred story has the power to shape the individual into the likeness of Christ, it also calls out a collective people, unleashing them in the world with the humble love and holy passion of God.

lectio divina

Another way to submit to Scripture as a means of grace is through the ancient practice of *lectio divina*. Latin for "divine reading," it opens a way for us to step into the story and let the story flow out of us. We are shaped by the Word and respond in obedient action. Because Scripture is the living and active Word of God, we are invited to not only read it, but engage and experience it. Lectio divina guides us in that journey through the following four stages.

31

lectio. The first step is reading Scripture. More than just letting our eyes pass over words, this is an active reading—taking the words into our hearts and minds. What words or phrases come alive and grab you? What thoughts do you trip over? In this moment, you may decide to read the passage or selected verses multiple times. You may even read out loud to engage your voice and ears along with your heart and mind. How does this change or enhance what you are seeing, speaking, hearing, and processing? Where are the sharp edges in these sentences? What statements or ideas convict, inspire, reveal, and encourage?

meditatio. The second movement is meditation. In this stage we reflect on what we read. We soak in the words, swimming down in the depths of them, until the Scripture sinks into our souls. In meditation we dwell in the Word and let the Word dwell in us. Mediation is an active waiting. We sit in silence and listen for God to speak through these sacred, breathing texts. We chew on truth and seek to understand the meaning of what is being revealed.

oratio. This third stage is marked by dialogue with God. After reading and seeking to understand the texts, we now respond in prayer. Oratio is the act of opening ourselves up to God, expressing to him the thrill, frustration, wonder, and questions sparked by this passage. We might engage this time by thanking him for what the text revealed. Or we might voice our confusion over its elusive meaning. But the point is that we pray in response to Scripture. We ask for guidance in how to internalize and act on it. We ask what changes need to be made in our relationships, private lives, attitudes, and ingrained habits. As the process of meditatio turns over the soil in our souls, oratio gives voice to the thoughts being unearthed.

contemplatio. The fourth step in this journey is contemplation. After reading through, meditating on, and praying over the passage at hand, contemplatio waits for direction on how to live this out. In meditatio we wait to understand what the text means. In contemplatio we wait to understand what it means to and for us. In other words, it asks the question, "Now what?" What are we asked to do in response? We've felt the truth, but what does this truth ask of us, here and now? What does God want me to do with this? This process is not complete until we act on it. Do not be misled by the thought that contemplation is merely a mental exercise. The practice of lectio divina culminates in our active obedience to the leading of the Holy Spirit through this journey.

further guidelines for reading scripture

John Wesley, founder of the Methodist movement, lived a life that sparked radical change in individuals and society. Historians agree that his ministry led to a spiritual awakening in eighteenth-century England, and at the same time, likely saved it from a violent cultural revolution. His sharp intellect fueled a hunger for reading widely and writing prolifically. Yet he often

referred to himself as "a man of one book." He under-
stood the power of Scripture and rooted himself in it.
He left behind several wise guidelines for reading
Scripture. Below is a paraphrase.

practice daily. We should get into the Word every
day. By submitting to this discipline, we become
rooted in Scripture, and it takes root in us.

go small. Wesley advises the reading of one chapter
per day, or even part of a chapter. By moving through
small portions at a time, we are able to focus our minds
and hearts more intentionally, and soak in what we are
reading.

listen and obey. He encourages us to read with the
focused purpose of knowing the whole will of God
and a fixed resolution to do it. Ask for wisdom to
know God's will and courage to obey it.

follow the story. The great themes run like a thread
through the Bible. Keep watch for them. How does
the passage at hand point to the larger story?

pray. As said before, the same Spirit who inspired
the Bible's writers then also enables the Bible's readers
now. Begin your reading with prayer for understanding. End your time with prayer for application and
transformation. Ask that the seed of truth will give
way to the fruit of growth.

pause and act. When finished, we should pause and
reflect on what we have heard. Then, in humble obedience we should actively live it out.

now what?

To assist you in the formational practice of Scripture, we suggest several steps for you to explore as an individual and in the context of a larger group.

We have provided you with a daily reading plan (at the end of this chapter) that follows the previously listed guidelines. This plan starts with the gospel of John, which tells the story of Jesus. It moves into Acts, the story of the early church, and Philippians, a letter to some of the first Christians from the apostle Paul. It then begins from the beginning of the Bible and covers the grand sweep of the great story.

This guide challenges you to read one chapter of the Word per day for six months (184 days). As a bonus feature for those who desire to dig deeper, it also includes one selection from Psalms or Proverbs for each day.

reflect

Being an active reader of God's Word, both individually as well as in community, is a primary way that connects us with the kingdom and ways of God.

For practice, read Genesis 1 aloud with emotion and creativity. Read each word with precision and intentionality. Don't rush through it as if you are reading an e-mail from a friend, but rather become part of the story. Imagine the scenes, smells, and creation that is being formed.

Now read Psalm 19.

What has God revealed to you through his Word? What images, faces, illustrations, or lessons is he currently revealing to you?

consume

When we do not learn to handle Scripture—to read, hear, and experience God's Word in its entirety—we rob ourselves and those around us of indispensable truths that God has made available, truths that cannot be obtained by humans on their own.

Spend time memorizing a few passages. Plan some time in your day, to commit to training your mind and heart in memorizing these passages. Here are three passages to consider: Romans 8; Colossians 3; and 1 Corinthians 13.

Repeatedly read entire books of the Bible in a short period of time. Intensity yields great gains in spiritual growth. Start by reading Genesis 1 and begin to see God's story revealed.

Practice lectio divina, as described in this chapter.[5]

study guide

1. Is Scripture dead or alive? Is the Word active in you and in your faith community (small group or church)? How is it active or not active? Why?

2. Toward the beginning of this chapter we discussed Scripture being God's story of his love for humanity and his quest to rescue and redeem his creation. Read Genesis 1 and 3. How does your story connect and relate through these passages? Now verbally tell the story of God's Word and truth which is revealed in your story.

3. In this chapter, we discussed why we should read Scripture. From your own experience, come up with a top ten list on why we neglect to read Scripture.

4. In what environments are you able to connect best with God's Word? How can you create space in your schedule to find time to search Scripture in these environments?

5. Robert Mulholland speaks of a tension in reading Scripture as informational reading versus formational reading. Do you tend to read Scripture for information or formation? The two work best in unison with each other. How can you creatively read Scripture, gaining information, while also being transformed in mind and spirit?

6. Look back at the section on reading in context. When you read Scripture, do you read it in context (thinking about the environment, historical significance, setting, or background)? Take ten minutes and

do a quick study on John 4. How does your understanding of the truth of John 4 differ after your short
study? What truths, perspectives, or even new questions
came out of your study?

daily reading plan

1. John 1; Psalm 1	35. Acts 14; Psalm 35
2. John 2; Psalm 2	36. Acts 15; Psalm 36
3. John 3; Psalm 3	37. Acts 16; Psalm 37
4. John 4; Psalm 4	38. Acts 17; Psalm 38
5. John 5; Psalm 5	39. Acts 18; Psalm 39
6. John 6; Psalm 6	40. Acts 19; Psalm 40
7. John 7; Psalm 7	41. Acts 20; Psalm 41
8. John 8; Psalm 8	42. Acts 21; Psalm 42
9. John 9; Psalm 9	43. Acts 22; Psalm 43
10. John 10; Psalm 10	44. Acts 23; Psalm 44
11. John 11; Psalm 11	45. Acts 24; Psalm 45
12. John 12; Psalm 12	46. Acts 25; Psalm 46
13. John 13; Psalm 13	47. Acts 26; Psalm 47
14. John 14; Psalm 14	48. Acts 27; Psalm 48
15. John 15; Psalm 15	49. Acts 28; Psalm 49
16. John 16; Psalm 16	50. Philippians 1; Psalm 50
17. John 17; Psalm 17	51. Philippians 2; Psalm 51
18. John 18; Psalm 18	52. Philippians 3; Psalm 52
19. John 19; Psalm 19	53. Philippians 4; Psalm 53
20. John 20; Psalm 20	54. Genesis 1; Psalm 54
21. John 21; Psalm 21	55. Genesis 2; Psalm 55
22. Acts 1; Psalm 22	56. Genesis 3; Psalm 56
23. Acts 2; Psalm 23	57. Genesis 4; Psalm 57
24. Acts 3; Psalm 24	58. Genesis 6; Psalm 58
25. Acts 4; Psalm 25	59. Genesis 7; Psalm 59
26. Acts 5; Psalm 26	60. Genesis 8; Psalm 60
27. Acts 6; Psalm 27	61. Genesis 9; Psalm 61
28. Acts 7; Psalm 28	62. Genesis 12; Psalm 62
29. Acts 8; Psalm 29	63. Genesis 13; Psalm 63
30. Acts 9; Psalm 30	64. Genesis 14; Psalm 64
31. Acts 10; Psalm 31	65. Genesis 15; Psalm 65
32. Acts 11; Psalm 32	66. Genesis 16; Psalm 66
33. Acts 12; Psalm 33	67. Genesis 17; Psalm 67
34. Acts 13; Psalm 34	68. Genesis 18; Psalm 68

69. Genesis 19; Psalm 69
70. Genesis 21; Psalm 70
71. Genesis 22; Psalm 71
72. Exodus 1; Psalm 72
73. Exodus 2; Psalm 73
74. Exodus 3; Psalm 74
75. Exodus 4; Psalm 75
76. Exodus 5; Psalm 76
77. Exodus 6; Psalm 77
78. Exodus 7; Psalm 78
79. Exodus 8; Psalm 79
80. Exodus 9; Psalm 80
81. Exodus 10; Psalm 81
82. Exodus 11; Psalm 82
83. Exodus 12; Psalm 83
84. Exodus 13; Psalm 84
85. Exodus 14; Psalm 85
86. Exodus 19; Psalm 86
87. Exodus 20; Psalm 87
88. 1 Samuel 16; Psalm 88
89. 1 Samuel 17; Psalm 89
90. 2 Samuel 7; Psalm 90
91. 2 Samuel 11; Psalm 91
92. 2 Samuel 12; Psalm 92
93. Daniel 1; Psalm 93
94. Daniel 3; Psalm 94
95. Daniel 6; Psalm 95
96. Matthew 1; Psalm 96
97. Matthew 2; Psalm 97
98. Matthew 3; Psalm 98
99. Matthew 4; Psalm 99
100. Matthew 5; Psalm 100
101. Matthew 6; Psalm 101
102. Matthew 7; Psalm 102
103. Matthew 8; Psalm 103
104. Matthew 9; Psalm 104

105. Matthew 10; Psalm 105
106. Matthew 11; Psalm 106
107. Matthew 12; Psalm 107
108. Matthew 13; Psalm 108
109. Matthew 14; Psalm 109
110. Matthew 15; Psalm 110
111. Matthew 16; Psalm 111
112. Matthew 17; Psalm 112
113. Matthew 18; Psalm 113
114. Matthew 19; Psalm 114
115. Matthew 20; Psalm 115
116. Matthew 21; Psalm 116
117. Matthew 22; Psalm 117
118. Matthew 23; Psalm 118
119. Matthew 24;
      Psalm 119:1–40
120. Matthew 25;
      Psalm 119:41–88
121. Matthew 26;
      Psalm 119:89–136
122. Matthew 27;
      Psalm 119:137–176
123. Matthew 28; Psalm 120
124. Romans 1; Psalm 121
125. Romans 2; Psalm 122
126. Romans 3; Psalm 123
127. Romans 4; Psalm 124
128. Romans 5; Psalm 125
129. Romans 6; Psalm 126
130. Romans 7; Psalm 127
131. Romans 8; Psalm 128
132. Romans 9; Psalm 129
133. Romans 10; Psalm 130
134. Romans 11; Psalm 131
135. Romans 12; Psalm 132
136. Romans 13; Psalm 133

137. Romans 14; Psalm 134
138. Romans 15; Psalm 135
139. Romans 16; Psalm 136
140. James 1; Psalm 137
141. James 2; Psalm 138
142. James 3; Psalm 139
143. James 4; Psalm 140
144. James 5; Psalm 141
145. 1 Corinthians 1;
     Psalm 142
146. 1 Corinthians 2;
     Psalm 143
147. 1 Corinthians 3;
     Psalm 144
148. 1 Corinthians 4;
     Psalm 145
149. 1 Corinthians 5;
     Psalm 146
150. 1 Corinthians 6;
     Psalm 147
151. 1 Corinthians 7;
     Psalm 148
152. 1 Corinthians 8;
     Psalm 149
153. 1 Corinthians 9;
     Psalm 150
154. 1 Corinthians 10;
     Proverbs 1
155. 1 Corinthians 11;
     Proverbs 2
156. 1 Corinthians 12;
     Proverbs 3
157. 1 Corinthians 13;
     Proverbs 4
158. 1 Corinthians 14;
     Proverbs 5

159. 1 Corinthians 15;
     Proverbs 6
160. 1 Corinthians 16;
     Proverbs 7
161. 2 Corinthians 1;
     Proverbs 8
162. 2 Corinthians 2;
     Proverbs 9
163. 2 Corinthians 3;
     Proverbs 10
164. 2 Corinthians 4;
     Proverbs 11
165. 2 Corinthians 5;
     Proverbs 12
166. 2 Corinthians 6;
     Proverbs 13
167. 2 Corinthians 7;
     Proverbs 14
168. 2 Corinthians 8;
     Proverbs 15
169. 2 Corinthians 9;
     Proverbs 16
170. 2 Corinthians 10;
     Proverbs 17
171. 2 Corinthians 11;
     Proverbs 18
172. 2 Corinthians 12;
     Proverbs 19
173. 2 Corinthians 13;
     Proverbs 20
174. Ephesians 1;
     Proverbs 21
175. Ephesians 2;
     Proverbs 22
176. Ephesians 3;
     Proverbs 23

177. Ephesians 4;
     Proverbs 24
178. Ephesians 5;
     Proverbs 25
179. Ephesians 6;
     Proverbs 26

180. 1 John 1; Proverbs 27
181. 1 John 2; Proverbs 28
182. 1 John 3; Proverbs 29
183. 1 John 4; Proverbs 30
184. 1 John 5; Proverbs 31

3

prayer

a further mystery

Wendell Berry is a poet and farmer, both of which require the careful cultivation of living things. Some of his best fruit is found in a novel called *Jayber Crow*, the well-spun tale of a small-town barber. While in that universal crossroads known as college, the story's namesake finds himself wrestling with cosmic questions. And it feels like a losing fight. He carries this weight to the office of a wise professor and unloads his burden at his feet. The two share the following conversation, beginning with the professor:

"You have been given questions to which you cannot be *given* answers. You will have to live them out—perhaps a little at a time."

"And how long is that going to take?"

"I don't know. As long as you live, perhaps."

"That could be a long time."

"I will tell you a further mystery," he said. "It may take longer."[1]

Prayer is like that. It is riddled with mystery and alive with wonder. It fosters daunting questions that have confounded the sages. The point of this chapter is to try to answer a few key questions on the subject. But these pages will only be part of the journey to discovery. To move into a deeper understanding of this sacred practice will require us to live our questions out beyond this book. And that may take as long as we live. Or longer.

In light of the long road ahead, we'll start at the beginning with a foundational question.

what is prayer?

Prayer is, simply, communication with God. While it can be a conversation as intimate and comfortable as old friends, it goes beyond that. Sometimes prayer cannot be bound by words. It does not need the structure of complete sentences or even complete thoughts. At times it is expressed by unspeakable pain or joy beyond the reach of language. Other times it flows out of us like lyrics or lines of poetry, eloquent and articulate. But always, prayer is a movement of the heart—communication between a person and God. This communication finds various forms and avenues for expression.

asking

When thinking of prayer, our minds run first to the specific act of asking God for something. And if we are honest, we will confess that our prayers are heavy with this theme. At first glance, it seems utterly self-centered to burden down the privilege of prayer with our inward-focused requests. But this is in no way trivial. Do not feel guilty about asking God for something. In this act lies a profound amount of faith and humble trust. To ask is to profess belief in his power to accomplish it. Alive in the request is the acknowledgement that his is the help you need.

God invites us to honestly express our needs and desires to him and to actively trust in his strength and wisdom for the outcome. He welcomes our asking and collects our cares with the heart of a good and loving father. We ask for wisdom and direction when at a critical crossroads. We ask for help when we are drowning in debt or addiction. We ask for rescue when we can't find a way to freedom. We ask for protection for our children, healing when our closest friend is struggling with a deadly disease, or hope when our family is fractured by betrayal. We ask for divine action that runs the spectrum from minor to miraculous.

For many of us, this is where faith first begins. In desperation we turn to the last known possibility of hope. Flinging our circumstance out into the empty heavens, we wait for it to land on far-off ears. When God breaks in with an unexpected answer, we begin the journey of waking up to the strange possibility that God hears us and cares enough to act.

intercession

Intercession is praying for someone else. It literally means to intervene on someone's behalf or to step into his or her situation. In this prayer moves beyond the personal and becomes an act of community. This is the art of prayer as friendship, the hard and courageous work of fighting for each other in the trenches of need.

Intercession creates a shared ordeal, thrusting us into a story that is not our own. It connects us with the burdens of others and teaches us to carry them with a strange mix of joy and pain. It actively opens our eyes to the injustice and suffering in the world and dares us to do something about it. And while intercession itself is a noble action, it also has a way of inspiring and sustaining further waves of tangible involvement.

questioning

Prayer can also come in the form of questioning. This is not to be confused with asking. In asking we make requests and approach God with our needs. In questioning we bring our doubts to him. We express our fears. We verbalize our internal turmoil. In asking we are looking for action, but in questioning we are looking for answers.

Let us be clear: God is not afraid of our doubts. He is not offended by our questions. At times our souls boil with rage, and our minds run on rants when we experience pain and suffering. Personal pain is hard enough to deal with, but perhaps the most difficult is when we are forced to watch helplessly as someone we love walks a broken and lonely road. "Why me?" is easier to answer than "Why her?" or "Why him?"

In times like these, God welcomes our questions. We assume that to give voice to our questions is to announce our lack of faith and renounce our trust in him. This is not always true. After all, to question God requires enough faith to believe that he actually has an answer. It is, in some strange way, a subtle declaration of hope.

What waits for us is not always clean, neat answers. Instead, it is the mind of Christ, the heart of the Father, and the strong comfort of the Spirit. So maybe our questions are not barricades in the path, but more like guides for the journey. Maybe they invite us, even dare us to search the discoverable mysteries of God, pressing us beyond the shore and the shallows and out into deep water.

worshiping

Prayer often finds itself taking on the form of worship. In this we express our gratitude to God for what he has done in our lives and the world, and we praise him for who he is. This kind of prayer focuses our hearts and minds on the greatness and goodness of the Father, Son, and Holy Spirit.

As we practice this pattern of prayer, the action of worship is no longer restricted to a particular building on a particular day at a particular time. Instead, worship

47

infiltrates our every move and orients us into this epic story of redemption that God continues to write in the world.

This type of prayer is foundational to the others mentioned here. As we rehearse God's greatness and reflect on his attributes and character, we undergird our asking, intercession, and questioning with a sense of God's faithfulness. When we remember how God came through in one situation, it gives us hope in the middle of the next difficult season. It reminds us of how real and strong and able he has proven himself to be. Worship rightly resets our frame of reality because it consistently retells the story of who God is and what he has done.

fasting

Fasting is both a physical and spiritual form of prayer. It is the act of denying oneself (usually food) in order to focus more completely on God. Understand this first: Fasting is not a spiritual hunger strike. History remembers several honorable hunger strikes that advanced great causes. They have been used to pressure political powers, raise global awareness, and stir the public to action. But fasting is different. It is not designed to capture God's attention, win his favor, or sway his sympathy. Instead, it is a submission of our cravings—even those that are the most primal and necessary. Fasting is designed to focus our attention on God, not focus his attention on us.

A misguided view here can give birth to an abusive, unhealthy understanding of how we please God. Is he so self-absorbed or distant or indifferent to us that we have to starve ourselves to get him to move? Must we hurt ourselves to gain his attention and affection? No! Our names are always on his lips and our faces are always on his mind. Fasting is instead a reminder to us that he is our source of fulfillment. It is a recalibration of our cravings—a shift in desire from us to him.

why should we pray?

Why should we pray? The answer to this second question is found in the first. We should pray because it is communication with God, a way for the finite to connect with the infinite; a means of grace by which the created can commune with our creator. And as we know all too well, the quest to do exactly that is as old as Adam.

prayer as communion

From the moment humanity lost the paradise of harmony with God in the garden, our souls have instinctively labored to lead us back as if, innately, humanity longs for God. Rarely are we honest enough to say as much, so instead we label ours a search for meaning or beauty or goodness. But what we are looking for is what we lost long ago—God.

This is why we should pray. Prayer connects us with the one who created us, the one for whom we

49

were created. Through his grace, he has initiated the redemption and restoration of what was lost. Prayer is an expression of that. Sin forced us out of God's presence, but prayer is an open invitation back in. Sin put God out of our reach, but prayer draws us back into his heart. In the invitation and action of prayer, what the whole world chases is found. Therefore, prayer in and of itself is an answer to our most deep and desperate plea—to be one with him again.

prayer as transformation

Who would expect to encounter God and walk away unchanged? To discover what the human soul has always desired and step away as if nothing significant happened? To come in contact with and experience connection to God is to taste transformation. This is another reason why we should pray: to find ourselves changed by his love and shaped by his heart.

In his classic book *Celebration of Discipline*, Richard Foster says, "Real prayer is life creating and life changing." He continues, "To pray is to change. Prayer is the central avenue God uses to transform us."[2] This process of change begins when we open our hearts to him, voicing our desires, dreams, fears, and needs. The essence of this action is submission and trust. We are saying that we need him, and that on some level we understand he alone can help us. In this small submission, we find the first seeds of change. But these seeds of change are cultivated into saplings of transformation when we move beyond voicing and begin to listen.

prayer as listening

Thomas Merton once shared this observation with a friend: "How does an apple ripen? It just sits in the sun."[3] It is tempting to strive and hustle our way toward advancing growth in the inner life. But we must remember that organic and healthy growth will include quieting our hearts and submitting to the slow and subtle process of spiritual formation. It calls for sitting in the sun and receiving the often undetected nurturing and cultivation that come from the vine.

Be still. Slow down. Listen. Don't give up because you don't hear a thundering word from the sky or a clear command in your mind. Open your heart to hear from God through the living voice of the Bible. Watch for his face in the forgotten corners of your city. Experience his beauty in the world around you, exploding with artistic whispers of revelation. Hear from him in the everyday avenues of your life.

how should we pray?

It would be foolish to talk about how to pray without starting with the most obvious and trustworthy answer, the one given by Jesus himself in Matthew 6. In his Sermon on the Mount, Jesus sat down on a hillside, opened his mouth, and reshaped the world. In the thick of radical ideas about loving our enemies and reversing the order of the blessed, he offered a simple and humble approach to prayer. He said, "This, then, is how you should pray" (Matt. 6:9). With those words, all of our attempts at defining and explaining prayer should grind to silence as we lean in and listen.

the hypocrite

Jesus began his curriculum on prayer with pointed instruction on how not to pray. In Matthew 6:5, he warned us not to pray like the "hypocrites" who impress with their performance but tragically miss the point. They have mastered the mechanics of prayer, but beneath their full and flowery language hides an empty heart. Their goal is to be "seen by men" rather than heard by the Father.

In *The Divine Conspiracy*, author Dallas Willard points out that the word *hypocrite* is lifted directly from classical Greek terminology for a stage actor.[4] Not until Jesus used it Matthew 6 did the word carry any kind of moral meaning. He pulled this term from common life to show the nature and character and lack of depth in the actions of many religious practitioners. Actors play a role, a momentary embodiment of a character, but they are not really the person they portray on stage. Yes, actors can be convincing and even bring great conviction to their work. But in the end, no matter how passionate the performance or valiant the execution of the craft, the curtain always falls. The actor always leaves the stage and sheds the role. As the applause fades, so does the feigned love of the hypocrite. Jesus says not to pray like that. God is not listening from a box seat, waiting to be entertained or moved to action. This is our Father we are talking to. We should be ourselves.

our Father

Jesus gave a model prayer in Matthew 6:9–13. He traced the heart of authentic communication with God. Interestingly enough, it begins with an earthbound concept of an intimate family relationship. In a profound move of grace, Jesus pulled us into this divine Father-Son intimacy that he experiences with God. Throughout the Gospels, he hammered away at the idea that God is his Father. But in this passage, he instructs us to pray, "Our Father."

This changes everything. Prayer is no longer a futile attempt to win over a far-off deity, but trusting our hearts to a good and loving Father who wants what is best for his children. For some, this image opens up prayer, infusing the practice with a new sense of freedom, security, and hope. But for others, imagining God as a father instantly shuts off and strangles any ability or even desire to relate to him at all.

Many people have an incredibly difficult time believing in and grasping the idea of God as a father. Because of real-life experiences and unshakable disappointments, this image falls dead on some hearts. Failure on the part of a father is so deeply painful and utterly scarring. It is because we know, innately and instinctively, that it should be different. The ache is there because something deep inside whispers to us what a father should be like. But when reality tells a different story, the hurt runs deep.

But herein lies the beauty of Jesus' gift. Somehow we know what a father should be like, and now we can experience the unexpected reality of that in our heavenly Father. Some people dream of what it would be like to have a father who cared, protected, stayed, believed, and loved. We can let our dreams run wild. We still won't come close to imagining how good this dad is. He is everything we've ever hoped for and he has the power to heal all the scars and restore the broken places. He is the best kind of Father, brimming with goodness and mercy and love. Jesus, in kindness and grace, frames everything else he says about prayer with this foundational thought about exactly what kind of God we are praying to: We can approach him like the good and loving father we've always wanted.

your will be done

Jesus walked us deeper down the path of prayer by instructing us to ask for the Father's will in Matthew 6:10. Having been shown his heart, we should now trust his design. Once again, this is an invitation into submission. It is a posture of the heart that signals surrender to the wisdom and dreams of God.

It is easy to imagine Jesus teaching on the hillside of Matthew 6, astounding the crowd with his authority and eloquence. To hear him say, "Your will be done" in this setting is one thing. But now flash-forward to the night-covered garden. On the last night of his life, he was burdened with the weight of his mission. The reality of the cross was moving over him like a gathering storm. Broken, he pled with his Father to let this cup pass from him. Then, with resolve and surrender he prayed, "Yet not my will, but yours be done" (Luke 22:42).

From the comfort of the hillside, Jesus told us how to pray. But beneath the shadow of the cross he showed us. Out of a heart of submission, he asked for and embraced God's will above his own. In this dark scene, we learn a lot about prayer. We see how Jesus prayed, but we also catch a glimpse into how God answers.

in Jesus' name

Jesus taught us that God is a good and loving Father who desires the absolute best for us and wants to "give good gifts to those who ask him" (Matt. 7:11). But does this mean that God will respond to every request with yes? Not necessarily. The best kinds of dads know when to say no. Jesus pled for the cup of suffering to pass from him. But God did not answer this prayer in the affirmative. Jesus himself knew the sting of "No." Hours later, however, this "No" to

Jesus' deliverance morphed into an eternal, sweeping, swelling "Yes" for us. Had Jesus escaped the cross, we would still be slaves to sin.

Jesus taught us to pray in his name, saying that when we do, what we ask will be given to us (John 14:13–14). Doesn't this guarantee God will answer, bound by this promise? Is "in Jesus' name" a foolproof formula for successful prayer?

Some have been misled to believe that we can somehow corner God and force him into action by simply mentioning these words, as if we can use the name of his beloved Son to manipulate him into serving us. These are not magic words for getting what we want ("open sesame," "abracadabra," "in Jesus' name," "amen"). Instead, to pray in his name is to establish the framework for a surrendered heart.

To ask in Jesus' name is ultimately to ask for his will. When a king's name is stamped on something, it is a sign and symbol of his reign, his realm, and his rule. If his name is on it, then his authority is over it. In the same way, when we pray in Jesus' name, we ask according to the ways of his kingdom. We fix his name over our prayer and place our prayer under his jurisdiction. To pray in his name is to pray in line with the overall framework of his heart for us. We ask for what we want but trust that he will give us what we need.

now what?

To assist you in the formational practice of prayer, we suggest several steps for you to explore as an individual and in the context of a larger group.

follow the forms

This chapter opened with the exploration of several forms of prayer. We discussed asking, intercession, questioning, and worshiping. Try to use the forms as a framework and pattern for your daily prayers. Spend time each day intentionally engaging each form.

As an example, as we learned in this lesson, an intercessory prayer pleads to God on behalf of others who desperately need his intervention. Today, lift up the people and situations that God brings to mind. Allow the Holy Spirit to suggest the people, nations, causes, and situations to bring before him.

get creative

Find a way to creatively express your prayers that fits your personality, gifts, and passions. This could include journaling, poetry, art, activism, or building something. If this seems weird to you, don't worry about it. Never feel pressured to express yourself in a way that doesn't fit who you are. Remember, this is your Father you're talking to. Be yourself.

pray with Jesus

We know we should pray to Jesus, but what if we tried to pray with Jesus? Search through the Gospels and take note of the places where Jesus prayed. What did he ask for? How did he pray? What poured out of his heart and stirred in his mind? Walk with him in his school of prayer. Pray with him.

fast

Choose one meal to give up during the week. Since patterns can be helpful, we suggest a fixed day. Set aside the time you would normally spend eating for prayer. When you feel hungry, use that as a reminder to focus your heart on God. Ask him to be your strength and to nurture a deeper hunger in your soul for him.

fast with friends

Invite friends to join you in your fast. This cannot be forced or coerced. But if you are in a small group or some other form of faith community, encourage them to walk through this with you. Let fasting become a shared experience for your group. You might find yourself being drawn closer to each other as you are drawn closer to God.

posture prayers[5]

Throughout the history of the church, Christians have not prayed just through the means of words, but by raising their hands (praise), kneeling (honor), bowing (requesting), and other means of integrating the physical with the verbal. For example, "for pray-ers in the first century, it was common to pray facedown with one's knees pulled close to the chest and one's forehead touching the ground. Doing so put one close to the ground and in the most humble position possible."[6] Explore by practicing these three postures of prayer. First, with your palms facing up, plead with God, seeking to receive his grace and love. Second, relax the muscles in your face and begin to smile, and ask God to help you be a blessing to someone. Third, kneeling on the floor with your head facing toward your knees, your eyes closed, and your palms covering your mouth, cry out to God, interceding for the poor and those who have no voice. Think of the oppressed, victims of human trafficking, abused, and refugees and displaced people across the world. Cry out and plead for justice, mercy, and restoration.

Now think of other creative ways to integrate physical and verbal prayers to experience God's presence in a unique way.

design a prayer room

Spend one of your small group gatherings creating and walking through a prayer room. You can set up different stations in your living room or at your church. Designate a specific station for each type of prayer discussed earlier. Add your own forms to the list as well. Get creative in your design.

study guide

1. Do you find praying difficult, or is it a practice that comes easily to you? Why?

2. In what ways do you normally pray—silently, in groups, over meals, in a quiet time, throughout the day, or other?

3. Prayer is a movement of the heart, and this communication between a person and God finds various forms and avenues for expression. What forms do you typically practice? Think outside the norm. What are some other creative ways you can pray?

4. Prayer sometimes comes in the form of questioning. Remember that questioning is different than asking. Do you find it difficult to bring God prayers of doubt, fear, and internal turmoil? Is it difficult for you to ask God questions? Discuss.

5. Prayer connects us with the one who created us and for whom we were created. It is an expression of restoration, drawing us back to his heart. Do you ever ask yourself why you should pray or if it is even worth it? Discuss with some friends why we pray. What answers did you come up with? The next time you pray, relax, listen, and just be, allowing your prayer to connect both your mind and heart. Let God do his work in you.

6. Read Matthew 6:9–13, the passage on Jesus' instructions on how we should pray. Pray each segment of this prayer, dwelling on each word. If you are in a group, break up the passage and pray it together.

What is God revealing to you through this prayer about him and about you? Discuss.

7. There is something supernatural and revealing when someone calls you by name. What do you think is significant about praying in Jesus' name? When you pray, do you verbally state his name in your prayers? Try fixing his name over your prayer. Verbally say, "Jesus," inviting his presence by calling on him. Try humbly closing your prayer time by affirming the Godhead, the Trinity, "In the name of the Father, Son, and Holy Spirit. Amen."

8. Do you tend to pray for God's will to be done or your will? What is his will? Read Matthew 6 on praying his will. Reflect. Remember. React.

9. What creative ways can you pray with others? Make a list, and through your creativity, allow his Spirit to meet with you.

4
worship

I (Matt) will never forget the image. In the balcony of the church in Centerville, Ohio, she was lost in worship. But that is not what makes the moment unforgettable. My mother-in-law Mary Ann loved to worship. Hands raised and heart full, she was passionate about her Savior and faithfully expressed it from every corner of her life. This was normal. Nothing new.

But what sets this particular day apart is that nothing else around her was normal. Weeks earlier, she had been diagnosed with an aggressive form of brain cancer. Months later, it would take her life. Her entire world was shifting, sliding off its foundations. Her family and church were reeling, unable to hold back the coming future. Everything was falling.

And yet, there she was. Hands raised, heart full, lost in worship as she sang the lyrics, "Oh no, you never let go. Through the calm and through the storm."[1] Was she just trying to escape from the stark, fearful reality for a few emotional moments? No, she was being drawn into the more real reality of our story. The storm was still very much there. But so were the strong and faithful hands that would carry her through.

This is what authentic worship does. It reorients us in the greater story. It draws us into reality. It enables us to see the world as it really is.

what is worship?

worship is reality

Richard Foster captures this idea when he says, "To worship is to experience Reality, to touch Life."[2] It is not a momentary, experiential escape from the difficulties of the real world. Instead, it is a clear-eyed recognition and declaration of the ultimate reality.

Worship establishes in our hearts and souls the undeniable framework through which everything operates. It reminds us that there is only one God and his name is Yahweh. He is the undisputed king of the universe, the creator and keeper of all things. He is in absolute control. If he were to remove his hand from us for even a moment, the whole show would spin out of control and into destruction. He is God. He is Father, Son, and Holy Spirit—distinctly three, yet the one and only. He is great and good, loving and holy. He is everything true, everything real. Because of this, we give him our undivided praise, our full-hearted worship, our entire selves.

Joan Chittister, Benedictine nun and spiritual teacher, says, "Worship is the natural overflow of those who, with humble and grateful heart, understand their place in the universe and live in awe of the God who made it so."[3]

Worship reveals to us the world as it really is. It pulls back the curtain on the chaos and brings into focus the one who is making things right. It puts tragedy and pain into perspective. It instills humility and thankfulness while moving us into our proper place. It illuminates a wildly powerful God who loves with an untamed fury.

This is not an escape from reality, but a revelation of reality. Worship is like saying, "Yahweh is God. He is in control, and I belong to him."

worship is response

It was another particularly moving worship experience. Through the music and the message I (Matt) was taken off guard by the depth of God's love for us. His far-reaching grace and reckless love engulfed me in a fresh and surprising way. At the close of the service, our friend John Freed stood up to pray. In this prayer, one line stood out, capturing everything I was feeling. He said, "God, we love you too."

And there you have it. That is the essence of worship. It is our response to what God has done and who he is, like saying, "I love you too."

Again, Richard Foster finds a way to help us understand. He writes, "It is God who seeks, draws, persuades. Worship is the human response to the divine initiative."[4]

God always initiates. He creates, speaks, promises, intervenes, sends, and calls. He even steps into human history himself, becoming one of us. God always makes the first move.

Theologians refer to this as God's "prevenient grace" or "grace that goes before." As mentioned in an earlier chapter, John Wesley described it as "the first light of dawn in the human soul." You might also call this awakening grace. The point is, God has always been drawing us to himself. Worship is our response to this love that has been calling our name. Worship answers back, "I love you too."

why should we worship?

Well, the answer to that question is obvious enough. But let's explore the idea a bit. In his book *Ancient-Future Time*, Robert Webber says that we gather together for worship for three central reasons: to remember God's saving action in history, to experience God's renewing presence, and to anticipate the consummation of God's work in the new heavens and new earth.[5] The true worshiping community engages in memory, experience, and anticipation.

worship as memory

The first and most obvious reason for worship is to praise God for who he is and what he has done. His attributes and actions spark a response of awe, reverence, and love. One of the most important purposes for worship is to remember God's saving acts in the history of humanity.

Ancient Hebrews commemorated his acts by setting aside special, holy days (such as Passover and the Day of Atonement). These celebrations not only involved retelling the sacred stories of deliverance and protection, but they usually consisted of some type of ritual reenacting of the event. Through touch, taste, and action, they would reconstruct the seismic events that shaped them as a people.

In the same way, we gather to retell the rich history of our salvation. Historically, the Christian church is tied to a common calendar, letting set seasons guide us through the journey of our redemption.

During Advent we hang on the well-worn words of ancient prophets, waiting for the arrival of the promised Messiah. At Christmas we marvel at the humble majesty and mystery of the incarnation—God becoming flesh in Jesus. In Epiphany light reflects off the truth that hides right before our eyes. Through Lent we fast as we walk with Jesus down the dreaded road that ends at a cross. On Good Friday we mourn the darkest day in history and contemplate Christ's sacrifice. Easter Sunday morning shakes us awake with the impossibly good news that "He is risen! He is risen, indeed!" On Ascension Day we hear his promise to return and our command to go. And Pentecost sends us out in the strength and power of the Holy Spirit, making the new boundaries of the kingdom anywhere disciples dare to go.

These markers of time are like anchor points constantly rooting us deeper in our own story. They help us remember. And rather than growing stale with lifeless repetition, they actually hold the potential to add layer after layer of meaning to our ever-expanding experience.

worship as experience

Worship remembers God's saving acts in the world. It also brings that past into the present as it helps us experience his renewing presence now.

We experience God's renewing presence in worship in a myriad of ways. His presence is alive in the reading of his Word, each page on fire with inspiration, imprinted with his heart and mind. His presence fills our prayers, collecting each one, delighting in our voiced and silent trust. And he revels in the sound of our rising songs. Perhaps we feel his presence so strongly in music because it has a way of communicating to him our inmost feelings. It is the expression of what is happening deep inside. He must love that.

Another powerful and mysterious way that we experience his presence in worship is through the sacraments: Communion and baptism. These visible words bring theology to life right before the eyes of the Christian community. Here, memory and experience overlap in an inseparable manner.

In Communion, also called the Lord's Supper or the Eucharist, we celebrate Christ's death on the cross

67

for the forgiveness of our sins. On the night before his crucifixion, Jesus shared a special meal with his friends. As the disciples joined him around the table, Jesus took bread and broke it. Then he told them that the bread represented his body that was being broken for them. Taking the cup, he said that the wine symbolized his blood that was being poured out for their salvation. To this day, Christians everywhere still share in this meal, reenacting and retelling the events of this Last Supper. Each time we celebrate Communion and remember Christ's sacrifice for us, his presence is alive in it. The Holy Spirit assures us that our sins are forgiven through this extravagant act of love. As the bread and cup pass our lips, his robust mercy dances on our tongues. This is tangible grace.

The same is true in baptism. The water stirs meaningful memories of God's deliverance of his people. It brings to mind his faithfulness to Noah through the flood, the parting of the Red Sea for Moses, and even the baptism of Jesus himself. But most importantly, baptism mirrors the pattern of Jesus' resurrection. Just as he died and was buried in the grave, we also die to our old lives of sin as we go under the water. And just as Christ was resurrected from the dead, we too are raised up to new and eternal life. This is what baptism represents. And every time someone comes up out of that water, soaked in grace and drenched in forgiveness, God's renewing presence is alive in that act.

In each of these elements, God's presence is alive. But there is still another vital place where his presence is active in worship: within us. You may not feel God's presence in the music or message, or in the bread or cup. But never forget that as a believer in Jesus Christ, you have been given the gift of the Holy Spirit. The presence of God is always with you, dwelling in you.

Throughout the Old Testament, God's presence dwelt in a tabernacle, a temple, or on specially commissioned servants. But as the New Testament unfolded, the story took a shocking turn. Through the incarnation, God came to dwell not only with people, but as a person. He became one of us. Then at Pentecost, his presence was on the move again, this time filling every follower of Jesus. His presence is no longer located in a centralized place of worship. Now it is swelling up and spilling out into the streets, empowering a grassroots movement of kingdom expansion. Every place we set foot becomes a new frontier of his mission. In this, worship sends us out to engage the world, empowered and emboldened by this presence inside of us. As our good friend Kerry Willis puts it, "His breath in my bones. That is the plan." This is the genius of God at work in us. Perhaps this is what Rabbi Abraham Heschel means when he says, "To worship is to expand the presence of God in the world."[6]

worship as anticipation

In worship we remember God's saving acts in the past and we experience his renewing presence now, but we are also drawn to look ahead. Worship anticipates what is yet to come and sends us into the future with unflinching hope.

Scripture teaches us that one day God will finally and ultimately set all things right and make all things new, that the day is coming when Christ will return for his people. The book of Revelation records a vision of the future that God is creating and paints the picture in these shades of hope:

> Then I saw a new heaven and a new earth, for the first heaven and the first earth had passed away, and there was no longer any sea. I saw the Holy City, the new Jerusalem, coming down out of heaven from God, prepared as a bride beautifully dressed for her husband. And I heard a loud voice from the throne saying, "Now the dwelling of God is with men, and he will live with them. They will be his people, and God himself will be with them and be their God. He will wipe every tear from their eyes. There will be no more death or mourning or crying or pain, for the old order of things has passed away." (Rev. 21:1–4)

In the end there will be a new beginning. The Holy Spirit continues to whisper this hope to us. We are assured that the deep scars left by our fall will be wholly healed and the crippling effects of our sin will be reversed through redemption, that the battle has already been waged and the victory has been claimed. The enemy is defeated. And Jesus is the last man standing.

Ours is a forward-looking faith, optimistic about the future and moving boldly toward it. But we must walk with corrective caution here, remaining fully engaged with the present. Heaven should be our hope, but it should not become our obsession. While God will one day restore all things, we must recognize that he is already about that very work in the here and now. And, in a shocking twist, he invites us into this work alongside him, shaping the future through our acts in the present.

"Kingdom come" is not a far-off place. It is already beneath our feet, breaking into the world. As our friend Jo Anne Lyon once prayed, "May we see God's future kingdom invading the present." We look ahead with a certain hope. And we engage the world, letting that kingdom break in through us, here and now.

how should we worship?

in spirit and truth

When exploring the ways in which we should worship, we turn first to the answer Jesus gave. In John 4, Jesus was conversing with a woman from outside of his traditional religious framework. She asked him about the proper forms of worship: Where was the right place

71

to worship? Jesus, in his typical fashion, cut through the issue of mechanics and unearthed the real heart of the matter. He said, "Yet a time is coming and has now come when the true worshipers will worship the Father in spirit and truth, for they are the kind of worshipers the Father seeks. God is spirit, and his worshipers must worship in spirit and in truth" (John 4:23–24).

This does not mean forms and styles are not important. They are. Misguided practices in worship can form false, harmful, and even destructive ideas of God. Forms and styles matter. But what matters most in worship is spirit and truth. God asks for the sacrifice of engaged spirits and authentic hearts. When this is what we bring into worship, then ancient liturgy burns with fresh life; innovative styles are layered with depth.

With this in mind, we should avoid demonizing forms and styles that differ from our own tradition. We should recognize and celebrate the potential that exists in each for the expression of engaged spirits and authentic hearts. We should humbly learn from the experience of others and embrace the diversity that thrives in the church, born out of the heart of this ancient and creative God.

creative expression

Creative expression should be encouraged within the church. We are made in the image of an infinitely creative God. With an artist's eye, he paints the landscape, sculpts the canyons, and composes the symphony that sends stars dancing across the sky. When we awaken and express this creativity, we are speaking his language.

For centuries art played a central role in Christian worship. The church commissioned masterpieces, classics that continue to capture the imagination. How did we lose that? Let's make the church a hub for creativity and art in our culture again. Let's make our faith community a place where the inner artist is awakened, empowered, and released.

Historically, the breathtaking works of stained glass that grace the windows of our churches and cathedrals actually served as a way of communicating the salvation story to worshipers. As the sun shines through them, intricate images of grace and mercy come alive in the light. So what will become our new stained glass? What art forms will emerge as a way of telling the story in creative ways? Art and beauty have a disarming quality that allows the walls to come down. Simultaneously, beauty draws us in. It is compelling. It invites our participation and our interpretation of the truth that lives within it. Art and beauty are stunning avenues through which we are challenged to respond to what we see.

with surrendered heart

In Romans 12:1, Paul urged, "In view of God's mercy, to offer your bodies as living sacrifices, holy and pleasing to God—this is your spiritual act of worship."

To worship in spirit and truth means to become living sacrifices to God. In our culture, sacrificing means to give something up, usually involving emotional or financial discomfort. But remember the context in which Paul wrote these words. When Paul chose the word *sacrifice* to describe worship, it had a different kind of weight and significance. Fresh out of a religious system where animal sacrifice played a central ritual role, this word was tangled up with graphic and gruesome imagery. It did not mean to give something up. It meant, bluntly, to submit to the painful process of dying to our selves. Worship calls for all-out abandon. It asks for a fully surrendered heart with nothing held back. It warns us that this might just cost us everything.

in context of community

Worship is intensely personal, but it is not an individualistic or isolated affair. The practice of remembering, experiencing, and anticipating should be a shared act within the context of a larger community. God wants each of us to live with sacrificed hearts. Jesus calls each of us to decide for ourselves to come and follow him. And the Holy Spirit fills and empowers each of us from within. But the triune God is simultaneously shaping a collective people. He is crafting a worshiping community, held together and bound to one another by an uncommon, self-giving kind of love. When we come together for worship, we are drawn in to a unity that comes from a shared story and sent out to creatively express it through our unique lives.

practicing the presence of God

While the regular gathering together for community worship is vital, it is important to remember that worship is not restricted to one hour one day a week. It is not centralized in one building. It works its way in and through every part of our lives. We walk in the constant presence of the Father, Son, and Holy Spirit. The challenge is to recognize that presence alive within and around us, engaging with him in the ongoing discipline of conversation, praise, and prayer.

C. S. Lewis said, "The world is crowded with Him. He walks everywhere *incognito*. And the *incognito* is not always hard to penetrate. The real labour is to remember, to attend. In fact, to come awake. Still more, to stay awake."[7]

Brother Lawrence, who lived nearly four hundred years earlier, said, "We should establish ourselves in a sense of God's Presence by continually conversing with Him."[8] And later he wrote to a friend, describing the joy he experienced in this practice, "There is not in the world a kind of life more sweet and delightful than that of a continual conversation with God. Those only can comprehend it who practice and experience it; yet I do not advise you to do it from that motive. It is not pleasure which we ought to seek in this exercise; but let us do it from a principle of love, and because God would have us."[9]

now what?

To assist you in the formational practice of worship, we suggest several next steps for you to explore as an individual and in the context of a larger group.

reflect

Take a moment and think about these questions: What or whom do you cherish? What or whom do you value? Take some time to reflect on those names or things. Write them in your journal or on a piece of paper.

Worship reveals what is important to us, and worship happens when we intentionally respect and honor Christ above all else in life. Therefore, as you proceed in the exploration of creatively practicing worship, keep his Spirit first. John 4:24 states that, "God is spirit, and [we] his worshipers must worship in spirit and in truth." Meditate on these powerful words, evaluating your life. In what ways is your spirit worshiping his Spirit in truth? Is he honored by your thinking and actions? Does your life worship and seek first his kingdom, keeping other things secondary? Do you give your whole self—thoughts, feelings, attitude, intellect, and will—to him, or is there a part of you that still remains your own?

Do you tend to be negative toward the peripheral things of the worship service (the sound, style of song, sermon)? Do you hold the opinion that worship is centered around a certain hour of the week when we "do" church? How do you think God's Spirit can change those attitudes?

Take some time to evaluate your heart as you think about the power and reality of worship. Ask yourself, "Am I giving God my all, focusing and responding to him with my whole being?"

As you engage in these next steps, allow your worship to be focused so that your spirit adores, loves, and honors his Spirit.

memory

Haddon Robinson says, "Worship without study is fluff; study without worship is sin."[10] In this light, slowly read Romans 1:21–26. After your first read of the text, pause, and take some time savoring every word that the apostle Paul wrote. Repeat these steps seven times (read, relax, and reflect). Allow your spirit to resonate with the Spirit of the Word.

After the seventh reading in response to the Word, express your thoughts through journaling or drawing. Allow this study to be a time of authentic worship through the reading and study of his Word.

Reflect on the times when you have been really moved in worship. What do you recall being the reason for this impact? Was it a certain song, being outdoors, a certain passage in Scripture, or the people you were around? Try to find ways to recreate those spaces and moments, and ask God to meet with you there again. You'll come to realize that even though God does meet with us in unexpected locations, he is a familiar God, who has given you sacred spaces to return to. The question is, are you claiming those places as sacred? Remember them, claim them, and return to them ready to worship.

experience

Through song, word, meditation, and interacting with fellow believers, delight in the Lord. It might seem uncomfortable or difficult at times, but keep practicing. Remember, it's not so much about being a master of the practice as it is being a faithful student.

In worship, whether at church, home, or out in his creation, try responding through all five senses. We typically respond and experience God through hearing and speaking, but what about the other three? How can you worship and respond through touch, taste, or sight? Explore ways to worship and respond to him. Here are a few ideas to start.

taste. Create a meal that centers around the passage, like a seder meal, or a food that is in the passage you read, like unleavened bread. You'll typically find that when it comes to taste, much preparation, thinking, and time is required. Therefore, much will be learned.

sight. If applicable, respond to what is going on in your soul by painting or drawing. What is God saying to you?

Try preparing the room where you have devotions, small group, or worship in a way that welcomes the

Spirit of God. Be intentional with the space. Do the aesthetics and environment seem inviting? Do they speak to the holiness and reverence of God? What about contextually? Does the environment also speak to what God is doing in your context?

smell. Incorporate different smells using candles or incense. Even the smells from food or coffee can enhance the worship experience. Maybe a passage describes a perfume or oil used in ancient times that you can use, extending the reality of God's presence being as real today as it was then.

No matter what you do, let your creative juices flow and bring others along with you on this transformational journey of worship. Respond to how your spirit is connecting with Christ's Spirit.

Since God reveals himself to us in worship, visit a worship service with a different tradition or style than you are used to. In this experience, ask God to allow you to see through the worshipers and different elements of the service, revealing something new about him.

anticipation

Sometimes waiting and worshiping is met by a special, visible presence of God. However, in a culture that demands so much of our time, presence, and thoughts, anticipation can easily be met by frustration. The speed of God is different than the speed of humans. It is in the simple act of slowing down and waiting that the present is experienced to its full.

79

Pause, close your eyes, and imagine the reality of
the Holy Spirit with you here now. Fill your mind and
heart with the wonder and mystery of Christ and his
Spirit. Anticipate!

study guide

1. How do you define worship? Try an experiment. Ask five people how they define worship. Write down their answers and compare them. Are there any similarities between your own answers and the answers of those you asked? Any differences?

2. Do you think the church today has limited worship? Are there ways we can expand our worship? Discuss.

3. Read Romans 12 and make a list of the ways the apostle Paul described worship. How might your life, church, or community look different if you worshiped in the way described in Romans 12? List, discuss, and apply.

4. In what ways have you prevented yourself from practicing God's presence? Have you been caught in the trap of restricting God's presence to one hour one day a week, or maybe just experiencing his presence while in a particular building or setting? In what ways can you expand your experience of God's presence?

5. Based on your reading in this chapter and through the various Scriptures mentioned, is worship depicted as a private practice or communal practice? In what ways is, or can, worship be practiced in private? In community? Be creative. Don't limit your answers to what first comes to mind or what might seem like the easiest. Lose yourself in the creativity and see what God reveals. Share your practices and ideas or discover what others are doing at www.facebook.com/awakeninggrace.

5
mercy and justice

Mike sat across the table, talking back through his journey, the twists and turns that led a once-successful restaurant owner to the desperation of life in a homeless shelter. His eyes moistened behind the bold black rims of his glasses as he recalled his past. He ran his hands back and forth through his thick white hair, a visual reminder of just how long and winding the road had been.

Mike was moved, but the emotion he displayed seemed to have little to do with his own bad choices or unfortunate breaks. Instead, his voice cracked when he talked about the compassion he experienced after arriving at the shelter. For as long as he could remember, he had openly rejected Christianity as a religion for the simple-minded. He was opposed to it on intellectual grounds.

"But now here I am," he said. "And I cannot get past the fact that every bit of help I have received since landing here can be traced back to people motivated by Christian love. And there's got to be something to that."

Mike is right. There is something to that.

Although the doctrines of our faith can be defended and explained through sound reason and solid apologetics, the authentic expression of this faith seems to move a step or two beyond reason. The purely unreasonable idea of selfless and self-sacrificing love cuts through the most guarded opposition. Perhaps this is why love has been called "the new apologetic." The most eloquent articulation of Christianity comes in the form of active, emptying love. Ours is a compelling story. God searches out the least and the last, and to the shock of everyone, moves them to the front of the line. This faith hangs on a reckless love that gives itself away.

what is mercy and justice?

The thing about love is that it seems to be restless. It refuses to politely stay put. When a person experiences the transforming love of Jesus Christ, it has a habit of working all the way through that person, touching every single corner of his or her life. And it doesn't stop there. Love continues to run wild through that life until finding its way out into everyday, common expressions and actions. Love starts in the deepest places of the heart but quickly gets to work on an escape plan. It wants to break out of us and spill over into the broken places of the world. This love often manifests itself through avenues of mercy for the broken and justice for the oppressed.

83

Mercy has been defined as active and practical help, motivated by love. Mercy is love springing into action. It refuses to remain an innocent bystander in a hurting world. Mercy responds to brokenness with compassionate care and healing. Justice is also born out of love. Dr. Cornel West creatively described it this way: "Never forget that justice is what love looks like in public."[1] In other words, love manifests itself as fairness and justice when it shows up in our court system, in the laws passed by our government, and in the policies adopted by our schools and workplaces. Love, dressed in the work clothes of justice, rolls up its sleeves, fighting to ensure that fairness trumps favoritism. It speaks up for the voiceless and lends its strength to the powerless. You cannot legislate love. But you can and must act with justice toward those who feel the sting of injustice.

Mercy and justice are wrapped up in our spiritual experience. They are, in fact, inseparable from it. These good works do not produce salvation and holiness. But they are, without a doubt, the genuine products of salvation and holiness.

a compatible contradiction

As we use the terms *mercy* and *justice*, we must understand that they are not interchangeable ideas. They are intertwined yet distinctly different. They are separate yet need each other to form a complete, holistic kind of love.

Mercy and justice are alike, but they are not the same. They are two sides of a single coin. They are partners in an intimate and intricate dance, each taking the lead when appropriate. They embrace. They kiss. But they are not the same. They are a beautifully compatible contradiction.

Justice is fair. Mercy is anything but.

Justice sets things right. Mercy sets things free.

Justice establishes equality. Mercy unleashes extravagant love.

Justice wins our rights for us. Mercy gives us more than we deserve.

Justice is sharing the wealth. Mercy is emptying the purse.

Justice is concrete. Mercy is mysterious.

Justice is the cause. Mercy is the motive.

Together, they bleed into each other as a call to set right the laws of man, while setting loose the love of God.

why should we practice mercy and justice?

a reflection of God's heart

Injustice and brokenness are scars and fractures that can be followed all the way back to the fall. They are rotting fruit, born from the seed of sin. In the same way, mercy and justice are the ripple effects of redemption. They roll out and rise up like a tide of grace triggered by the reality of salvation. They are the pounding echoes of the heartbeat of God.

Throughout the story of Scripture, we see God's heart for the poor, outcast, and oppressed. The central narrative of the Old Testament reveals a God who hears the cries of slaves and actually does something about it. His prophets couldn't help but proclaim his desire for mercy and justice. Isaiah said in poetic fashion, "The Spirit of the Sovereign LORD is on me, because the LORD has anointed me to preach good news to the poor. He has sent me to bind up the brokenhearted, to proclaim freedom for the captives" (61:1). Later, Jesus used this passage to launch his ministry on earth. In his first sermon, he lined himself up with these words, establishing the framework for what his ministry would be about.

Amos declared, "But let justice roll on like a river, righteousness like a never-failing stream!" (5:24). Micah summed up what God requires of his people: "What does the LORD require of you? To act justly and to love mercy and to walk humbly with your God" (6:8). God cares deeply about the plight of the forgotten. As we practice mercy and justice, we step in rhythm with his heartbeat.

authentic worship

We also practice mercy and justice because they are our authentic expression of worship. Twice in the book of Matthew, Jesus was challenged by the Pharisees because he stepped beyond the bounds of respectable religion. Once, he was eating with a group of outcasts with well-earned reputations for questionable character.

Another time, he was healing a man with a shriveled hand on the Sabbath day. In both cases, Jesus answered his accusers by quoting the prophet Hosea. He said, "Go and learn what this means: 'I desire mercy, not sacrifice'" (Matt. 9:13).

The Pharisees were experts at obedience, but they missed the heart of authentic worship. To reflect God's heart is to become intentionally aligned with the very people no one else will stand beside. It is to throw in your lot with the broken and enter into their pain.

After all, isn't this what God did in the incarnation? Jesus stepped into our world, entered into our pain. This is where we continue to find him. As the poet Flannery O'Connor put it, "You will have found Christ when you are concerned with other people's suffering and not your own."[2]

to love God is to love others

When Jesus was asked to describe the greatest commandment, he summed up every command in one: To love God with all you have and all you are, and to love others in the same reckless, ridiculous way. Everything we have ever learned of God, he said, hangs on this (Matt. 22:36–40). True love for God will, without fail, give way to true love for others. Genuine concern and active compassion are sure signs that love is taking root in us.

To love God is to love others. But, by some mystery, it also works the other way. To love others is to love

God. Jesus taught us that whatever we do to the least of these, we also do to him. He is so present in the suffering of the weak, that acts of love shown to them are actually acts of love shown to God.

E. Stanley Jones captured this mystery: "And to the heart that has learned to love Him it is irresistible to think of Him hungry, thirsty, sick, in prison, naked, a stranger in the throbbing needs of our brother men. We take them Christ—we go to Him. He is the motive and the end."[3]

how should we practice mercy and justice?

The question of how to practice mercy and justice is a thrilling one, precisely because it has an unlimited range of answers. Love, being the energy at work in the creation of the universe, has the potential to reveal itself in the most creative ways. For a starting place, it might be best to explore a few examples from church history to recount the stories of how Christians in the past have expressed the love of God through mercy and justice toward their neighbors.

william wilberforce

The deep faith and Spirit-inspired convictions of a young William Wilberforce (1759–1833) thrust him into a fight that would define his life. From his seat in British Parliament, he struggled against overwhelming odds to put an end to Britain's slave trade. Pushing through defeat and the accompanying discouragement,

Wilberforce finally succeeded in his efforts, seeing the deplorable practice abolished.

john wesley

John Wesley (1703–1791), one of our shared spiritual heroes, is best known as the founder of the Methodist movement in England. A prolific writer and preacher, he traveled countless miles on horseback proclaiming a theology of "holiness of heart and life." Apparently, he was listening to his own sermons. This theology of love for God and others moved beyond the pulpit and into his personal life. John, his brother Charles, and the people known as Methodists, developed an inspiring ministry to the poor and oppressed throughout England. They founded clinics for the sick and lending systems for the poor, established education programs, and created employment opportunities. The Wesley brothers and their Methodist friends did not do this because they were activists but because they were Christians. They believed in the gospel that had given them hope, and they followed the teachings of Jesus all the way to their natural conclusions.

orange scott and luther lee

The legacy of Wesley made its way across the pond to our own shores. Around the time of the American Civil War, a small collection of courageous activists and abolitionists began to speak out and stand up against the practice of slavery. Led by pastors like

Orange Scott and Luther Lee, this remnant was soon forced out of the Methodist Church. In response, they formed the Wesleyan-Methodist Connection (a blatant and pointed nod to the ideals of Methodism's founder, Wesley). Some of their churches served as stations on the famed Underground Railroad, an intricate route of escape for runaway slaves.

They were for freedom from slavery. They were for equal rights for women (rights that stretched from the voting booth to the pulpit). They were for the kind of heart holiness that wells up and runs over into the most mundane and magnificent expressions of mercy and grace.

the booths

William and Catherine Booth founded the Salvation Army in the late 1800s. According the organization's own account of its history, "Thieves, prostitutes, gamblers, and drunkards were among Booths' first converts to Christianity."[4] Yes! Now that is a ministry résumé. William and Catherine were driven to love the oppressed, poor, hungry, and homeless of London. Their legacy lives on in the organization they founded. The Salvation Army continues to embody the marriage of mercy and justice, fueled by the unbridled love of the Father, Son, and Spirit.

modern-day inspiration

This passion for justice and compassion still burns in Christianity today. In many ways, we are experiencing a renewal and return to these roots.

We are inspired (and believe you will be as well) by stories unfolding as we speak. Some we have heard about from a distance. Some we have seen up close, through the lives of close friends committed to live out the self-giving love of Jesus in the context of their communities.

Josh founded and leads The Bridge Project which is called to be a prophetic witness of personal holiness, racial harmony, and social healing in Asheboro, North Carolina.[5] Adopting a single neighborhood, Josh and his family are, indeed, building a bridge into the hearts of at-risk teens, fatherless children, and a community that feels as if hope moved out a long time ago. Similarly, our friend Matt started The LOT Project in Anderson, South Carolina. Matt's contagious compassion has stirred college students and churches to join him in tangibly loving the poor and forgotten of his community.

And then there is David, Lane, and David. These college students courageously lead a group called H.O.P.E. (Homeless Outreach and Poverty Eradication). They wear that name well. While classmates are exploring the more common adventures that college can offer, these students are searching the streets on cold winter nights, armed with hot chocolate, warm coats, and blankets. Through monthly community dinners, they design intentional opportunities for local residents to share a table with their homeless neighbors. They also work tirelessly to strike at the systemic roots of homelessness and poverty, offering micro loans for small business start-ups. They even teach creative writing workshops and publish a literary magazine that features the poetry, short stories, and photography of their homeless friends.

Pastor Greg and his family have given their lives to ministering to one of the poorest areas in Indianapolis, Indiana. Their conviction and commitment to loving and transforming their community has created opportunities for unity through biblical hospitality where true transformation of lives can occur. Changing city policies through their advocacy work; feeding fifteen hundred people at Thanksgiving; and providing a safe place where prostitutes, drug addicts, and the forgotten are loved and given favor, Greg has given people a place to admit imperfections and brokenness, and experience healing and conversion.

Abby raises money to provide medicine for children in the Sudanese village of Wadupe, so they can stay in school. Amanda organizes gift bags, filled with messages of priceless worth and embracing love, to deliver to exotic dancers in New Mexico. Allison stands up for the issues and needs of a poor neighborhood that most of her town has either forgotten or doesn't know exists. She is putting it back on the map in the hearts and minds of the community. And Marci inspires college students and mobilizes churches to fight human trafficking, the modern-day slavery. Diverse actions sparked by a unified motive: to unleash the creative love of Jesus through tangible acts of mercy and justice.

These stories should inspire us. They should remind us of the church's rich heritage of embracing the broken and standing for the oppressed. But they should also drive us to do something. Rabbi Abraham Heschel said, "To understand love it is not enough to read tales about it."[6] Love must be experienced and expressed. To know love is to actively give it away.

now what?

To assist you in the formational practice of mercy and justice, we suggest several steps for you to explore as an individual and in the context of a larger group.

examine

Who influences your heart, mind, and decisions? What voices influence your spiritual, political, and civil decisions? Who sets your agenda and motivates you to the point of action? Is it a news show commentator, a news magazine, a non-profit organization, your church, or a friend or family member?

Read James 1:27—2:1 and examine yourself. Think about the above questions. To better capture what is happening within your spirit, you might choose to journal, take a walk around your city, or just rest in his Spirit. Ask yourself, "Am I being moved by Christ's mandate of loving the least of these, or am I being moved by public and political influence?"

93

Ask yourself or discuss with a small group these questions: What are some ways that we are guilty of drawing lines between the acceptable people and those we deem unacceptable? Do Christians do this? Does the church?

How would recognizing the fact that God is at work in all people change the way we talk with others and interact with nonbelievers?

Why do you think people prefer to draw clear lines between themselves and those who are different from them? What would it look like for Christians to stop thinking of themselves as better than others? Envision how nonbelievers might respond if Christians stopped being preachy and instead started listening to the stories of how God is already at work in the lives of others.

engage

Mercy and justice not only speak out, but they act out. Some call this advocating or acting on another's behalf. Is it your desire to love and advocate for others, seeking their good, protection, and dignity?

Do you desire a love that breaks through emotion and self-gain, and sees the other? Are you fully engaged? Are you looking at your world through Christ's eyes? Here are a few ways that you can engage mercy and justice.

listen and watch. Mercy and justice means to include, not exclude. Does your life welcome and invite the stranger, the needy, and the oppressed? Maybe the needy or stranger is someone you know but his oppression is hidden. Creating space to act justly is difficult, and unfortunately, it seems few people in the lives of the hurting really listen to what they have to say or ask questions to show interest in what they're saying; thus people feel rejected and remain hidden. Commit yourself to hearing the complaints, stories, and issues of those you interact with, such as the store clerk, coworker, wait staff, or family member. Rather than waiting for an opportunity, be proactive and ask simple questions like: "How was your weekend?" or "Is your day going well?" When the person answers, listen and give an appropriate response. As the conversation progresses, you might be able to ask deeper questions, but don't force it. Create space in your schedule to meet together to include this person in your daily routine, perhaps wrecking your agenda, but fulfilling God's plan.

be aware. Familiarize yourself with laws and policies that shape your government's decisions. Do your laws and policies provide opportunities for those in need or hinder their advancement? Call your local and state government officials and voice your opinion.

be a conscientious consumer. Refuse to buy food or products that oppress, abuse, or take advantage of the poor, all on the behalf of economic gain.

be a good steward. How could you give or share your things with others? Can you open your home to assist and transition a refugee family? Can you volunteer in your community to teach English, advancing the quality of life for those in need? Can you take a group once a month to serve at the local jail and provide various training and educational opportunities?

be responsible. Treat your family, friends, and those around you impartially and fairly, living out of a life that is other-centered, not self-centered.

What steps are you willing to take so that the injustices of this world fit into your thoughts and life? One option is to investigate and explore opportunities to serve and advocate for those in your church and community. What needs are represented by your findings? Does your heart break or identify with one of these service or advocating opportunities? Think and dwell on these findings and pray for those impacted by the injustice and oppression.

show mercy. Avoid acting out in judgment and oppression. Resist the urge to keep track of wrongs. Instead, protect and create opportunities for peace and love rather than hate and division.

Choose three ways to show compassion (the love of Christ) to someone this week. After you make that list, share it with a friend or group and discuss your experience.

Start a small group or ministry at your church or with your neighbors, and pray for peace and justice issues.

study guide

1. From your own experience and knowledge, how do you describe an act of mercy? What about an act of justice?

2. In this chapter, we spent some time discussing why we should practice mercy and justice. Based on the readings as well as your own experience, does the world's perspective of how mercy and justice should be lived out differ from God's? Discuss.

3. Mercy and justice do not produce salvation or holiness. But they are, without a doubt, the genuine products of salvation and holiness. Do you struggle with knowing how to live out mercy and justice in your context? In what ways can you live out mercy and justice in your family, church, and community? Brainstorm ways with friends or in your small group.

4. Though not exhaustive, we have supplied you with a list of examples in how mercy and justice are alike, yet not the same. They are what we call a beautiful, compatible contradiction. Go back and read through this list. Do you see the necessary relationship between mercy and justice? What other compatible contradictions would you add to our list? Discuss.

5. We learned from the Old Testament prophets Amos and Micah that as we practice mercy and justice, we step in rhythm with God's heartbeat. So, practically, what does Micah 6:8 look like? Break down the verse and list ways you can live out and apply these truths to your context.

6. In this chapter, we looked at historical and modern-day figures who transformed culture because of living out a committed life of mercy and justice. Who in your life would you say is a modern inspiration? What would it take for you to be a modern-day inspiration? Read 1 John 3:17–18. How is God speaking to you today?

7. In light of this chapter, read 1 Corinthians 13:3. What would the ramifications be if you lived out this passage? What would your life look like? How might your community, city, or church be forever changed? Think, examine, and discuss.

8. What ways do you practice and live out mercy and justice? Share your practices and ideas or discover what others are doing at www.facebook.com/awakening grace.

6
sabbath

It was a busy week, full of stress and weariness, and worst of all, nothing was getting done. It had less to do with time management or overcommitment, and more to do with the "more than usual" interruptions and distractions that entered my life. I (Jeremy) felt like a runner whose legs were as heavy as lead pipes, and yet, with my sides burning and desperately gasping for air, I knew there were more miles and obstacles ahead. At home, my daughter Ava was trying to tell me about her day over dinner. Though I heard what she said, I was not listening. Ava put a little hand on either side of my face and turned it forcefully toward her as she said, "Daddy, please look at my eyes."

This is exactly what God intended for you when he created the Sabbath, an intentional and set-apart time where your sight shifts from the busyness, stress, and deadlines to resting and gazing into the presence of your Abba Father: a time for being in the midst of a life of doing.

It wasn't until I put everything aside and began to truly engage with Ava that I realized how much I needed a conversation with this three-year-old to realign some of my priorities. And it is in the intentional time spent in Sabbath rest that you'll discover nourishment for a thirsty part of your soul.

what is sabbath?

The idea of Sabbath (Hebrew *sabat*), meaning a dedicated time of intentional rest, comes from two key passages in the Old Testament. The first is the creation narrative found in Genesis 1 and 2. Having invested six days of explosive imagination and energy into the creation of the universe, God rested on the seventh day. In doing this, he established by his example a rhythm of work and rest. Just as he drew boundaries between day and night and established a difference between winter and spring, he also carved out markers of time for work and rest and weaved them into the very fabric of nature.

The second key passage is found in Exodus 20:8–11 and 31:14–17. Set against the iconic backdrop of Mount Sinai, Moses delivered to the newly freed and formed nation of Israel the divine law of God. A key piece of this legislation was the command to. "Remember the Sabbath day by keeping it holy. Six days you shall labor and do all your work, but the seventh day is a Sabbath to the LORD your God. On it you shall not do any work, neither you, nor your son or daughter, nor your manservant or maidservant, nor your animals, nor the alien within your gates. For in six days the LORD made the heavens and the earth, the sea, and all that is in them, but he rested on the seventh day. Therefore the LORD blessed the Sabbath day and made it holy" (Ex. 20:8–11).

This command was given to a nation of recently freed slaves who had been subdued by ruthless masters. These slaves had been taught that their only value was in what they could produce. Their ability to work was the reason they were kept alive. Generations of God's people were raised under this lie. Now he wanted to show them the truth about who they were.

the cycle of sabbath

In this law, God not only established a weekly day of rest, but a further pattern of grace, a larger cycle of Sabbath. The pattern began with one day out of every seven being set aside for Sabbath. But it continued with one year out of every seven being established as a Sabbath year. Just as the Sabbath day was designed as a rest from labor, the Sabbath year was a rest as well, only on a larger scale. It instructed the people to let the land rest.

For six years they would plant, farm, and harvest. But in the seventh year, the land was to lie fallow. God communicated that he cared about the health of all of his creation. He established sustainable cycles of work and rest to ensure this health.

101

Now get this—he went even further. The pattern of grace, this rhythm of rest, kept rolling out. God also mandated that after seven Sabbath years (forty-nine years), the fiftieth year should be set aside as a sort of hyper-Sabbath. He named it the Year of Jubilee. And rightly so, because every fifty years God commanded any land that had exchanged hands should go back to the original owner. Why? The land had been given as a gift, as a family inheritance from God to his children the Israelites. Each tribe and family within Israel was given land in this inheritance. The only reason anyone would sell this land would be if they were in a desperate financial situation. The threat of poverty would force some to sell their inheritance for their family to survive. The Jubilee year was designed to reverse the crippling effects of poverty, building hope for future relief. By creating this command, God declared that there would be no permanent poverty in his land.

The Year of Jubilee didn't only offer hope for those who had lost their land; it also offered hope for those who had lost their freedom. In a stunning act of grace and mercy, God built into the constitution of his kingdom this command: Every fifty years, as part of the Jubilee year, slaves must be set free. Those forced to sell themselves into servitude out of desperation were given their freedom. Jubilee planted in the minds and souls of these freed slaves the hope that bondage would never be their unshakable fate ever again. The fifty-year cycle meant that every Israelite could experience this within their lifetime. No matter what their circumstance, hope was hanging out ahead. Jubilee was an intentional attack on fear and despair, filling the future with the promise of rest and restoration.

Sabbath is hope that we are more than what we can earn or produce. This is a taste of green pastures and still waters. It is an invitation into a sustainable life, designed and modeled by God.

why should we practice sabbath?

We should practice Sabbath because it is a gift of grace to us. In his wisdom and kindness, God established a rhythm of rest by his example and invites us to participate in it. Hidden in its practice are reminders of who we are and revelations of who he is.

sabbath as identity

Practicing Sabbath reminds us of who we are and shapes our understanding of our own identity. It reminds us that we are more than our work, more than the sum of what we can produce. Sandra Richter explores this idea of identity in her book *Epic of Eden*. She writes:

Can you imagine what the gift of the sabbath meant to the Israelites standing at the foot of Mount Sinai? A few months prior they had been slaves. Slaves who had been born of slaves. Slaves whose only value was the quantity of

labor they could produce before their backs gave
way and their strength failed. . . . And now this
God, who has claimed them as his "treasured
possession," is announcing that one day out of
every seven will be set apart for rest.[1]

But too often, we forget that we are free. Instead, we
measure success by outdated and irrelevant standards
that are dismantled by our new reality. We lionize people who keep a frantically full work schedule, and then
shake our heads and whisper in disbelief when they
burn out and break down. Perhaps the shame on their
shoulders belongs to us for honoring the wrong things
and guilting them toward "greatness."

Our chronic unwillingness to slow down comes
from a spirit of competition and false sense of worth
found through our work. And it's quite likely that we
are fueled by the fear of what might catch up with us
if we let the pace slip. Hear Richter again: "This message is as necessary in this generation as it was in
theirs. In our driven, workaholic world, in which we
are trained to think that the only measurable value of
our lives is the quantity of labor we can produce before
our broken bodies are laid in the ground, our Creator
says, the essence of the one made in the image of God
is not work."[2]

Sinai has something to say: You are no longer
slaves, but free sons and daughters. You are not defined
by your work or measured by what you produce. Your

identity in this new reality hangs on who God is, not what you do.

sabbath as alternative story

Because time is such a governing force in our culture, it says something when you are governed by a different kind of time. How we function in and relate to time is one significant way to signal that we are caught up in a different kind of story—an alternative story with peculiar priorities.

To carve out regular and rhythmic periods of rest is a declaration of what is important to us. It is a clear demonstration of what we value and love. It even sends a message about who or what we trust.

Time is a precious commodity, consistently on the move. We therefore feel pressure to capitalize on every unit of it in order to accomplish the most with what we have. To surrender such a precious and fleeting thing to God is a radical and risky move of trust. It says we have more faith in him than we do in ourselves, that we worship the true God who provides what we need, not the false idols of wealth and achievement that are never satisfied. Maybe that is why Rabbi Abraham Heschel called the Sabbath "a sanctuary in time" and "our great cathedrals."[3] It is a sign and symbol of whom we worship. In this light, Sabbath should be seen not as time lost, but time redeemed.

sabbath as memory

The Jewish practice of marking time often involves remembering and even reenacting the activity of God in the world. When celebrating the Passover, for instance, Jews still participate in an ancient and active meal, rich with meaning and layered with history. Taste and touch help bring an old story back to life. And they don't simply talk about the awaited return of the prophet Elijah; they physically get up from the table and check to see if he is standing at the door.

The same is true for the Feast of Tabernacles. To commemorate the forty-year journey of the exodus through the wilderness, ancient Jews were commanded to sleep in makeshift tabernacles, or tents, to connect them with the acts of their ancestors. The mind and spirit are instructed together through this physical action.

The Christian faith inherited this practice of remembering through reenacting. That is why we tear the bread and drink from the cup. We literally get wet in baptism.

The Sabbath is another example of this. By practicing it, we actively remember God's grace toward us. The Sabbath remembers and reenacts the creation event. And in doing so, it reminds us of the God who, out of the love firing back and forth within the Trinity, calls all that we know into existence. We pause and reflect on the moment when he invented humanity and rejoiced over his best idea. We remember, with awe, that he created us in his own image. We rest, as he did and look back over the genius of his creative love and strength.

sabbath as rising action

The practice of Sabbath is a way to actively remember what God has accomplished in the past. But it is also a means for anticipating what God has promised to accomplish in the future.

Sabbath helps us reflect on the event of creation, but it also draws our minds and hearts toward the coming and ultimate restoration of all things—the new creation. It rekindles the hope that one day God will redeem the world once and for all; that what went wrong in the garden will be set right through Jesus. It is a recurring reminder that the fallen will be lifted up and the broken will be healed. It looks forward to the day when God will rest again. It is rising action in this drama, hoping for the climax and resolution of restoration.

how should we practice the sabbath?

remember the gift

We should seek to practice the Sabbath as a gift of grace not as a legal obligation. To become consumed with the mechanics of how to precisely and properly observe it is to miss the point entirely. Remember the Pharisees? When Jesus healed on the Sabbath day,

107

they were outraged. Looking beyond the miracle, they focused on the minor matter of legal infractions. They were offended and objected the fact that Jesus carried out his work on the instituted day of rest.

But we know that the Sabbath is bigger than this. And Jesus is bigger than the Sabbath. A spiritual practice can be a helpful way to express our love and worship to God. Sometimes it is even a commanded way to do this. But we must always remember that the practice is an expression of worship, not the object of worship. It is dangerous to confuse the two. (Note: When the meaning of a practice gets distorted, the thing to do is reclaim the meaning, not do away with the practice itself.)

cultivate a pattern

Break the cycle of work with a rhythm of rest. Carve out a regular day (or even part of a day) when you can participate in focused, intentional rest. Then guard that time. Ask a friend for accountability in keeping it. We were designed for this, and life works best when we engage with this gift.

trust

To deliberately and regularly step away from your work is a bold move of trust. While you are resting, someone else is working, possibly progressing past you. Unsettling isn't it?

But at the heart of this whole thing is a spirit of surrender, abandon, and trust. We submit to the sometimes counterintuitive ways of God. We trust his wisdom and actively give him our clients, academic rankings, projects, promotions, deadlines, start-ups, ideas, and dreams.

worship

Try setting aside Sunday as your day of rest. For many who serve in roles of ministry, this is practically impossible. The demands of this day make it the most stressful and draining of the week. If this is the case for you, pick another day.

But if Sunday works for you, give it a try. It gives you the opportunity to make community worship a central part of your rest. It allows you to find renewal in the presence of God and his people. It opens the chance to enter into worship with an uncluttered schedule and focused mind.

rest

Here's a wild idea: Use your set-aside Sabbath as a time to rest. Relax. Unwind. Take a breath. Resist the temptation to catch up or get ahead.

relationship

Invest this time in your most important relationships. Share the experience with your family or close friends. These relationships are designed to be life giving. Let them be that.

restoration

To rest doesn't necessarily mean to rigidly restrict all motion. You can do something with your time. Just be sure it is something that restores you and energizes your soul.

Read. Grab a fishing pole and head for the lake with your kids. Explore the local hiking trails with your spouse. Take a nap in your favorite chair. Play basketball with your friends. Discover the community farmers' market with your roommate. Or do nothing at all.

The key is not whether you fill or empty your time. The idea is to use that time for intentional rest and restoration.

now what?

To assist you in the formational practice of Sabbath, we suggest several steps for you to explore as an individual and in the context of a larger group.

In Genesis 1, God ceased to create on the seventh day. He rested, and we, too, are to cease, releasing our control and acknowledging that God is God.

reflect

Is it difficult for you to cease from doing? Are you always working and getting ready for the next task, or stressing over the fact that there is not enough time in a day to meet all the deadlines that are calling out your name? Does this sound like your life? Take a moment to pause, rest for a moment, and in this state of being, with your eyes closed, begin to dream of what it would be like to take a day to enjoy the work of God.

What do you see? What might this day of ceasing look like for you? What do you feel? Do you feel a sense of anxiety, not knowing if you have the time to pause and rest? Do you feel a sense of freedom?

Scripture tells us that we are to keep the Sabbath day holy. In other words, revere, protect, and honor this sacred day. However, it is difficult to set aside any large amount of time, let alone a whole day to just rest. Reflect for a moment. In what ways have you not honored this day? Revered it? Protected it?

be intentional

The way to keep Sabbath is by solitude and fasting, that is, stepping out of work and the self-imposed expectations of doing. How might you be intentional in taking advantage of Sabbath today? How might you be selfish with the day, the period of time where you cease and just be? Being intentional for you might be a time of refocusing your energies and thoughts, willfully choosing to create space where your spirit rejoices with the Holy Spirit. Could it be that the images that came to mind in the reflective section above were not merely dreams but a spiritual reality? Could it be that what you were seeing was a glimpse of what your spirit is hungering for—rest and intimacy with the Spirit of God?

111

engage

Mark 2:27 says, "The Sabbath was made for man, not man for the Sabbath." So, be intentional to create the space where you practice some of these spiritual realties. Spend your Sabbath outside, take a walk, or have a picnic. If you are married, rest together. Read Genesis 1 and rejoice in how God created us to be with him, but also with each other. Your Sabbath might be going to bed early the night before and sleeping in the next morning, allowing your body to awaken you instead of being waked by your alarm clock. If you cannot sleep in, take a nap in the afternoon.

Try eating a meal at home, around the table with family and friends. Invite folks to bring a favorite dish and enjoy each other's company. Share around the table how you see God presently active in your life and how he is transforming you. Take some time to celebrate each other by sharing how you appreciate each person and the God-given qualities that you see in each other.

Celebrate this day. Rather than letting the day go by without observing or acknowledging it, try doing something a little different, something that is unexpected. For example, take a bike ride, a hike in the park, or sit on your porch with your spouse or a friend and be with God—no agenda, busy preparations, or high expectations, being with the Father. Your attitude and obedience in being present with God will be extraordinarily beneficial to your soul.

Try saying a candle-lighting prayer. Begin the Sabbath by lighting two candles, representing the two passages of Scripture that commanded the Sabbath — Exodus 20:8–10, which describes remembering, and Deuteronomy 5:12–15, which uses the Hebrew word for observe.[4] Read these passages as you light the candles to remember and observe who created everything, and acknowledging the Lord as Lord. In the traditional Jewish home, the mother circles her hands over the candles three times, welcoming the Sabbath light saying, "Blessed are thou, O Lord our God, King of the universe, who has hallowed us by his Commandments and commanded us to kindle the Sabbath light!"[5]

There are many ways to honor the Sabbath. The question is, how will you honor this sacred time that has been created for you, his most prized and honored creation?

study guide

1. In what ways is Sabbath a foreign or familiar practice to you?

2. By looking at two key passages in the Old Testament, we addressed the idea of Sabbath being a dedicated time of intentional rest. The first, Genesis 1–2, communicates the establishment of Sabbath; and the second, Exodus 20:8–11 and 31:14–17, communicates the legislation to remember the Sabbath day. How do you currently remember the Sabbath day? Do you create space in your life to rest, giving God your time and energy, and giving care to your soul?

3. We are more than our work and more than the sum of what we can produce. Although the world puts a lot of stock and self-worth in one's career and work, followers of Christ know that we are not defined by our work or measured by what we produce. Our identity in this new reality hangs on who God is, not what we do. How does the new reality rub against your context? Would this idea of Sabbath identity be received well by those in your church, workplace, or community? Would it be difficult? Why? Discuss.

4. Rabbi Abraham Heschel calls the Sabbath "a sanctuary in time." In this light, Sabbath should not be seen or perceived as time lost but time redeemed. Discuss this idea of time lost versus time redeemed. How can doing nothing, or putting events, schedules, or work on hold actually bring redemption versus stress or restlessness? How might this new reality of

understanding Sabbath change how you think of the practice of Sabbath?

5. As Sabbath helps us reflect on the event of creation, it also draws our minds and hearts toward the coming and ultimate restoration of all things, which we call the rising action in the story of God, hoping for the climax and resolution of restoration. How do you see God already ushering in resolution and restoration to his creation (in relationships, nations, the earth, etc.)? List and discuss.

6. Resting doesn't mean to rigidly restrict all motion, doing absolutely nothing. But in doing something, we must act in such a way that it restores us and energizes our souls. Take some time and reflect on this statement: The key is not whether you fill or empty your time. How will you use the time for intentional rest and restoration? Make a list of ten ways you will begin this journey, ushering in the practice of Sabbath.

7. What ways do you practice and live out Sabbath? Share your practices and ideas or discover what others are doing at www.facebook.com/awakeninggrace.

7
creation care

When we begin to talk about care for creation, we must immediately address several questions. In approaching this issue, it's easy to get entangled and embroiled with political and personal tensions. It does not have to be that way.

The purpose of this chapter is to examine creation care from a biblical perspective. With Scripture and Christian tradition as our guides, we will venture to put forth a call that is consistent with the heart of God and the soul of our movement. As we will discover together, this is not simply a reaction to hot cultural trends. The church has been voicing this call for centuries. It runs through the pages of Scripture, the teachings of the early church fathers, and the convictions of the Reformers. This is not a new idea, but it is a vital one for our generation. And we must rediscover and reclaim our voice on the matter.

As a starting point, let's describe what creation care is not.

Creation care is not creation worship. Instead, it is an expression of worship for God because he created the world, called it good, and continues to show his love and care for it. Out of love for God, we treat all that he made with grateful respect.

Creation care is not pantheism. Pantheism is the false religion that sees God and nature as one and the same. In this view, creation is God and God is creation. We call that a clear falsehood. Genesis tells us that creation finds its origin in God. Paul told us that God continues to speak to humanity through his creation. But God and nature are distinct and different. He works within it but is above and over it.

Creation care is not a political agenda. Views on the environment often run along the lines of political affiliations and allegiances. Creation care is not an attempt to advance a particular party's values. It is an attempt to advance Scripture's values. It is a response to what the Bible teaches about our relationship with the created order of things.

Creation care is not the elevation of things above people. It does not advocate concern for nature at the expense of love for humanity. In fact, it encompasses an active love for everything God has made.

what is creation care?

Creation care is, simply, a form of biblical stewardship. It is our obedient response to the original command God gave to Adam and Eve in the garden at the outset of human history. In his creative strength, God imagined the cosmos and spoke everything into being. As the words rolled out of his mouth, the universe came into existence.

Trees stretched to the sky, fish swam in the deep, and wild animals pounded across the plains. Mountains took their proud place against the horizon. Rivers wound their way through the forests and cut paths through the valleys.

And it was good.

But it was not complete.

In the center of it all, God placed humanity and named us the crown of creation. We were given a unique place in this new world. Distinguished and set apart from the rest, we are made in God's image. While all of nature is a reflection of his creative power, we alone are a reflection of his image. You and I are the glory of God walking the earth.

Along with this blessing comes a mandate. Genesis 1:26–28 captures this gift and command in poetic fashion:

> Then God said, "Let us make man in our image, in our likeness, and let them rule over the fish of the sea and the birds of the air, over the livestock, over all the earth, and over all the creatures that move along the ground." So God created man in his own image, in the image of God he created him; male and female he created

them. God blessed them and said to them, "Be fruitful and increase in number; fill the earth and subdue it. Rule over the fish of the sea and the birds of the air and over every living creature that moves on the ground."

The God-appointed role of humans in the garden was that of stewards of creation. We are to care for it, rule over it, and always remember our relationship to it.

the role of ruler

Some contend that the Genesis mandate to rule over creation gives us the right to treat nature any way we please, always regarding our own comforts and desires while disregarding the destructive impact this has on our environment. We hold the rights of kings and queens and exercise dominion by divine decree.

But this understanding of our relationship to creation is ill informed and misguided, even if the image of ruler is the best expression of the Genesis mandate. After all, we instinctively know how a good ruler behaves, with care shown for the subject. A king who rules with no thought of the subject is no more than a tyrant.

Francis Schaeffer helps us see the idea of our dominion clearly. He said, "We are to exercise our dominion over these things not as though entitled to exploit them, but as things borrowed or held in trust. . . . Man's dominion is under God's dominion."[1] And he went on to say, "Our conscious relationship with God is enhanced if we treat all the things He has made in the same way as He treats them."[2]

Therefore, if we are created in the image of God, we should reflect his heart and mind. We should follow his lead and rule as he does—with compassion, humility, and care for his subjects. And if we are in right relationship with God, his care and concern for every living thing should pulse in us as well.

the role of steward

As Schaeffer said, our relationship to creation is better described as steward rather than ruler. A steward is entrusted with the care of something that does not belong to him or her. His or her responsibility is to the master, and the master's property. As Christians, we understand that the world and everything in it belongs to the one who made it. He entrusted it to us, and we should respond to this gracious gift by caring for it, not abusing it.

why should we practice creation care?

creation care as theology

The practice of creation care is a common-sense response to the most basic ideas of Christian theology. In this, it is a natural outflow of our faith. If we believe that God created the earth and called this creation good, it only seems natural that his people would care for it.

The entire narrative of Scripture opens with this idea. Our first glimpse of God shows him creating the universe out of divine imagination and holy love. Our initial understanding of him is formed in the fresh light of earth's first morning. He made order out of chaos. In the beginning, God created.

Not only does the Bible begin with this foundational truth, but the Apostle's Creed starts here as well. For centuries Christians have committed this ancient creed to memory, understanding it to contain the doctrinal essentials of our faith. Many communities still recite it together every time they gather for worship. And what is the first line of this common creed? "We believe in God, the Father Almighty, Maker of heaven and earth." Our entire concept of God, our bedrock doctrines, our starting points for making sense of him, all begin with the idea that he created the world we live in.

If this is where our faith begins, where our oldest stories and most trusted theology starts, shouldn't our next natural step be to praise him for his work, to treat it with respect and gratitude, and to take seriously the mandate to tend the garden? This is the reasoning behind the practice of creation care.

But what about the fall as it's described in Genesis 3? Doesn't this great disaster plunge nature into a broken state, setting it at odds with humanity and sealing its fate for destruction? We base the rationale for creation care on a command given in the garden when the original glory was still intact, prior to the current reality of our broken world. Doesn't our present condition change the picture?

Without a doubt, the effects of humanity's fall into sin are disastrous. Our rebellion sends shockwaves throughout the entire realm of creation, and nothing is left untouched and unscarred. Like humanity, creation is fallen. But, like humanity, creation will one day be healed. Scripture promises that all things will be redeemed and set right. The curse of sin has been broken and its reign is revoked. In Romans, Paul described a creation that groans along with us for redemption and longs to share in our salvation. God did not abandon humanity after the fall. Will he abandon everything else he made?

We often view the physical world as inherently evil, as a lost cause destined for destruction. We break it down along these lines: the physical is bad; the spiritual is good. Makes sense, doesn't it? The only problem with this way of thinking is that it's called Gnosticism, a heresy that was fiercely opposed by our spiritual ancestors in the early church.

They were against Gnosticism because the life of Jesus stands as a direct critique of this heresy. Rather than deem physical nature as evil, Jesus took on human nature, becoming fully human while remaining fully God. It is called the incarnation, one of the great mysteries of our faith. It was through this all-out engagement with the natural world that he accomplished our salvation. He was born, crucified, and raised from the dead, all with a physical body.[3] He stepped into creation to save it from the inside. As

C. S. Lewis put it, "In the Christian story God descends to reascend. . . . He goes down to come up again and bring the whole ruined world up with Him."[4]

creation care as heritage

It is easy to see creation care as a passing trend, as yet another attempt on the part of the church to be seen as relevant to culture. But this is not a new idea in Christianity. The renewed focus and revived energy toward this practice is actually a reawakening for us. As Christians, this is part of our heritage. Some of our greatest thinkers and boldest leaders have urged us to look to nature as a source of spiritual insight and inspiration.

Tertullian described nature as our teacher, nurturing us in the growing knowledge of God.[5] St. John of Damascus said, "The whole earth is a living icon of the face of God."[6] And early church fathers Augustine and Chrysostom, along with the great Reformer-theologian Martin Luther, together called creation a compelling book through which God is telling the story of redemption.[7]

John Wesley also recognized our special relationship and responsibility to the rest of creation, noting the intimate and intrinsic connection between all things that find their origin in God. He said, "I believe in my heart that faith in Jesus Christ can and will lead us beyond an exclusive concern for the well-being of other human beings to the broader concern for the

123

well-being of the birds in our backyards, the fish in our rivers, and every living creature on the face of the earth."[8]

Clearly, Wesley was not advocating a decline in our concern for humanity. One glance at his legacy of mercy and justice toward the least and the last cuts through that misunderstanding. Instead, he was trumpeting an ever-expanding capacity for care. As we are drawn deeper into the heart of the Father, formed into the likeness of the Son, and filled and sanctified by the Spirit, then our hearts and lives will reflect the active and overflowing love of God toward all he has made.

Creation care is not a new idea. It is a spiritual practice that the historic church of Jesus has taken seriously through the centuries. It is part of our heritage. And it should be part of our legacy as well. Our children and grandchildren will inherit the world we are shaping today. As we walk in obedience to our calling as faithful stewards, we follow in the footsteps of those before us and pass this gracious gift to those coming behind.

how should we practice creation care?

remember God's gift

124

Psalm 24:1 reminds us that "the earth is the LORD's, and everything in it." This is the framework through which we view our own interaction with the world.

Nature is a gift to us, fashioned by God. Although he gave it to us to enjoy, we can never forget that it belongs to him.

remember your role

The earth belongs to God, but he has appointed us as stewards of it. Our role is to take care of it and treat it with the same respect and love that the owner would employ. We view our actions of care toward the planet as acts of devotion and service to the giver of the gift. It is not that we serve creation. We serve the creator of it.

remember your neighbor

It is important to remember that our actions have an impact on others around us. Often, these effects are felt most by the poor and vulnerable in our community and world. The senseless pollution of rivers and lakes lead to sickness and preventable illnesses that plague the communities relying on these water sources. And this is not something relegated to remote places in the world. Take a moment to consider how your actions might impact others. In this, creation care also becomes an act of mercy and justice.

read scripture in light of creation theology

As we read through our Bible, we can take note of the role nature plays in Scripture. We can see God's heart for his creation bleeding through. What are trees used to represent? How do the prophets portray pollution of the earth? What about the imagery of streams, mountains, and pastures?

merge theology and practice

As mentioned before, our theology begins with God creating the earth and calling it good. Commitment to this theology is key to our understanding of God. It even spurs some Christians to call for the teaching of this view in our public school science classes. And yet there is often a strange disconnect between what we passionately say we believe, and how we actually act on that belief. If we believe God created the earth, and if we want others to believe it as well, our practices should affirm that. We should be at the forefront of efforts to care for what God created.

start small

We can make small changes in our lives. We can begin by recycling our papers, plastics, glass, cardboard, and cans. This will help to drastically reduce the amount of waste pouring into our community landfills. We can work to find ways to reduce our usage of water and electricity in our homes. We begin with the small steps and ask God to reveal the next steps for actively caring for his creation.

now what?

To assist you in the formational practice of creation care, we suggest several steps for you to explore as an individual and in the context of a larger group.

reflect

In the Old Testament (Lev. 25), we learn how God's people were to take care of the land, and the things that come from it (animals, plants, water).

Read or listen to the following Scripture verses in order: Genesis 2:15; Psalm 24:1–2; and Romans 8:20–21. How do these words about taking care of creation and redeeming his work resonate with your views on environmentalism, creation care, and stewardship of the physical world? Do you find tension or agreement?

Search your heart and think about your creation care and being a good steward of God's creation.

Go for a walk around your neighborhood or the local park. Breathe in the rich air, take in the beauty that surrounds you, and reflect on these questions: How might God view the resources you consume or use? How, or where, have you taken advantage of God by not being aware of his creation and natural gifts to us? Where might you have taken advantage of God's gifts to this world? How might your actions have displayed your dominion over the earth rather than being a good steward of it?

Take some time to actively reflect by searching websites related to creation care topics. There are a

127

few suggestions below. Another way to actively reflect is to dialogue with others. Post some ideas and issues on Facebook or Twitter and discuss your thoughts with a group of friends. No matter the venue, actively reflect and learn. You will be amazed as to what God will reveal to you.

Here are a few questions to actively reflect upon:

1. How do you feel about animal rights activists, vegetarians, factory farms, oil companies, green initiatives, and global warming?

2. Based on what you read in this chapter, how might God view your use of natural resources and due diligence in taking care of his physical world—his creation?

3. How might your actions lead to making the earth more like God's original garden of Eden?

participate

Grab a piece of paper and list ways you and your family or a group of friends can make the earth more beautiful. If this is new to you, begin in small steps. Write down a list of what you can do this week, and then expand the list to a month and then a year. Here are a few ideas to get you started.

plant flowers or a garden. Better yet, teach a group of kids how to plant and take care of a garden.

be a voice in your community. Use your voice to make your area more environmentally friendly through its laws and policies. Look through your community newspaper or online, join a community meeting or organization that is already established. Give Christ a voice in your community.

go small. Take the time to recycle or organize a carpool schedule with fellow coworkers or parents. Maybe your church or workplace could adopt a road and make it one of the cleanest roads in your town. Make a commitment to buy some of your groceries locally. Many communities now have farmers' markets that offer organic and locally grown produce, eggs, and meats.

start a creation care group at your church. Educate folks on what it means to be good stewards of God's creation.

take a walk. Thank God for the things around you: the air, rain, sky, and grass.

make a list. Think of five actions you can implement within the next five days. Here are ten examples to help you move in this direction:

1. Recycle or compost your trash.
2. Carpool or walk.
3. Turn off lights.
4. Advocate (be a voice) on local and national environmental issues.
5. Adopt a highway or local park.
6. Plant a garden.
7. Buy organic items (food, clothing, resources).

129

8. Use alternative energies.

9. Reuse your plastic grocery bags. Better yet, bring your own cloth grocery bags.

10. Start a community garden with your family and neighbors and share!

Now make commitments to actively care for God's creation. Here are five suggestions:

1. Take intentional measures to reduce the harm you personally do to the environment.

2. Encourage local churches and organizations to adopt policies and practices that minimize environmental damage and reflect good environmental stewardship.

3. Include environmental stewardship as a topic for teaching and discussion in your church, school, and workplace in order to be equipped to take action appropriate to the setting and context.

4. Advocate for public and governmental policies that will protect and preserve the environment.

5. Lovingly communicate that all of these efforts are motivated by love for God and a desire to steward what he has entrusted to our care.

For more ideas and ways to engage God's creation, check out these great resources:

- http://www.creationcare.org
- http://earthministry.org
- http://www.energystar.gov
- http://www.gogreenthebook.com
- http://theregenerationproject.org

study guide

1. Reread the section on what creation care is not and think how those misconceptions have negatively influenced the views of creation care for the church today. How have these misconceptions influenced how you think and practice creation care? Discuss.

2. We learned that the God-appointed role of humans in the garden was as stewards of creation, which means we are to care for it, rule over it, and always remember our relationship to it. How does your life reflect care for God's creation? How does your church reflect that care?

3. Francis Schaeffer said that our relationship to creation is better described as steward rather than ruler, for a steward is entrusted with the care of something that does not belong to him or her. Do you think and act more like a ruler or steward over God's creation? Why? Discuss.

4. Do you find yourself struggling with the belief (or were you taught that) the physical world is inherently evil, therefore, why care for it? Do you tend to think and live as if the physical is bad and the spiritual is good? Reflect on these questions. Examine your life and those that influence you, both people and institutions. Discuss.

5. Discuss C. S. Lewis's statement about the realities of God's interaction with his creation. Does this ring true for you?

6. What is your initial reaction when you hear someone talk about creation care? Do you think creation care

is a trend, driven by political agendas or misconceptions? Discuss.

7. Reread the "Creation Care as Heritage" section, which reflects on the lives of a few that have paved the way for us to carry on this message of creation care. What do these faithful stewards teach us today?

8. Reference the "How Should We Practice Creation Care?" section, and take some time to remember. Remember by reflecting on these sections, "God's Gift," "Your Role," and "Your Neighbor." Take what was revealed to you in this time of reflection and put them into action. Share with a friend or your group.

9. What other ways do you practice and live out the creative response of caring for God's creation? Share your practices and ideas or discover what others are doing at www.facebook.com/awakeninggrace.

8
covenant friendship

the golden sessions

There is something transformational about the nature
of friendship that can turn a moment into a memory. It
can lead hurt into healing. It can infuse impossibility
with an air of hope. Friendship has a crucial kind of
quality to it that makes the journey worth the work.
In his book *The Four Loves*, C. S. Lewis described
the gift this way:

> Each member of the circle feels, in his secret
> heart, humbled before all the rest. Sometimes
> he wonders what he is doing there among his
> betters. He is lucky beyond desert to be in such
> company. Especially when the whole group is
> together, each bringing out all that is best, wisest,
> or funniest in all the others. Those are the golden
> sessions; when four or five of us after a hard day's
> walking have come to our inn; when our slippers
> are on, our feet spread out towards the blaze and
> our drinks at our elbows; when the whole world,

and something beyond the world, opens itself to our minds as we talk. . . . Life—natural life—has no better gift to give. Who could've deserved it?[1]

Friendship touches a deep place within us. In a way, it forgets who we were, reminds us of who we are, and believes in who we can become.

what is covenant friendship?

To say that humanity longs for relationship and is incomplete in the absence of it is in no way a new thought. It is, in fact, one of the oldest stories in the book. It was one of the first truths discovered about us, while the dew was still glistening in the garden.

This innate need and desire is not a result of creation's early fall, and therefore rooted in some sinful or even slightly twisted self-focus. No, it was there from the beginning. In fact, Adam's lonely, pre-Eve state was the only thing not named as good in the creation narrative. The Trinity quickly fashioned a perfect companion for Adam, making the work complete. It was, therefore, part of God's original design for us. True relationship with another person is a faint echo, a flickering glimpse of who we were made to be. There is something truly pure and stubbornly good in it.

135

the root of relationship

Let's trace the origin further back and see just how deep this root will lead us. The seed of relationship is seen in the garden at the dawn of human history. But it is a reflection of a truth even older than this. In fact, we see the beauty of full relationship fired by love at work within God himself. He is community. The triune God is Father, Son, and Holy Spirit, existing as three in one since before the foundation of time, bound together by perfect love. Our desire to relate, to become one, is built into the bone. Written into our DNA is this reflection of who God is. Part of what it means to be made in his image is to be a relational being. We were made for community.

The Genesis narrative, then, does a number on our embedded values. In our culture, rugged individualism is a cardinal virtue. But individualism stands in opposition to the idea of true community because it values the self as first. It is an outlook that does not look out at all, but is turned inward, and is therefore distorted. Hear this clearly: God celebrates every individual, but he did not intend individualism. We are each different, yet made for unity. Every soul represents an utterly unique creation, and yet every soul is unmistakably linked to the whole of humanity. There is a sharp distinction between being unique and living alone.

covenant of communitas

The idea of community is crucial to the Christian experience. We were made to be part of something larger than ourselves. Because the word *community* has earned such a prevalent place in our shared vocabulary and may have lost some of its strength in the process, we have employed the term *covenant* to describe the depth of friendship we are talking about. *Covenant* is a word that captures the meaning of relationship and drags it below the surface until it crashes on the ocean floor. It has a sense of unshakable commitment tied to it. As the word passes your lips, you can almost hear the sound of the heavy door slamming shut and the locks clanging into place. You are in, and there is no getting out.

In *The Forgotten Ways*, author Alan Hirsch calls us beyond community and into "communitas."[2] Communitas is a level of relationship that a group experiences when its members pass through some sort of trial together. In the process, people are bound to one another by the struggle. Through the shared ordeal of a difficult road, they break through into deeper, more meaningful love and respect. Communitas emerges from the awareness that we need each other.

The idea of communitas calls to mind a group of friends united against incredible odds. This collaboration from diverse (and sometimes divided) backgrounds is fused by friendship, pulling together for a common cause. We are talking about a shared journey that is anything but safe and sterile. It is an epic quest, dangerous and messy, but the purpose is worth the price and difficulty. This goes way deeper than the

137

polite social gatherings we often associate with fellowship. This is something worth giving your life for.

Historically, communitas and covenant have marked the family of Jesus Christ. We are intimately joined together through the depth of our shared story, stretching back through the trauma of the cross and triumph of the empty tomb—the new covenant that binds us to Christ and each other. And we continue to lean forward together through the crisis of spiritual journey, through the persecution of our brothers and sisters around the world, and toward the stirring hope of the journey's end.

why should we practice covenant friendship?

We enter into the practice of covenant friendship because of the model of Scripture. Most notably, we see it embodied in the teaching and life of Jesus as well as in the actions of the early church. This rare breed of friendship is a thread that runs through the New Testament, serving as a distinguishing mark of our movement.

the command of Jesus

When Jesus was asked what the most important command was, he gave a brilliant answer that unites every command ever given: Love God with all you have, and love your neighbor as yourself. The second is a natural outgrowth of the first. Authentic love of God will always lead to genuine and generous love for others.

Jesus later said that love for others should begin within the body of believers. In John 13, while sharing his last meal with his disciples, Jesus said, "A new command I give you: Love one another. As I have loved you, so you must love one another. By this all men will know that you are my disciples, if you love one another" (vv. 34–35).

This seems somewhat counterintuitive. Wouldn't it be a more compelling story for the world if we loved those on the outside first? We are absolutely called to love the world in a way that points to Christ. But if we don't love each other, our boldest feats of mercy and justice are empty. You cannot love a stranger and hate your brother. Unity is stirring. The people of this world will believe in our love for them if they witness our genuine love for each other.

the example of Jesus

Jesus did more than teach on the importance of Christian community. He modeled it. First, he entered into our story and shared in our burdens. To think of the incarnation fills the heart with a strange kind of hope. It proclaims that God walks in our shoes and experiences every thrilling high and crushing low. His experiences are now tangled up with our own. He is not far off, but he walks the road with us. There is dirt on his hands and dust on his feet. Jesus laughed and wept. In the moment between the mystery and the knowing, John Wesley used his last breath to whisper

139

our first hope, "Best of all, God is with us." For the sinner there could be no better news than to find a friend like this.

It's like the story of the man trapped in the pit who turned to find that a friend had dropped down into the hole beside him. "Now we're both stuck," cried the man. With a knowing smile, the friend answered, "Yes. But I've been here before and I know the way out."

Selecting a shocking collection of unlikely followers, Jesus invited twelve to become his disciples. He poured his life into this eclectic, ragamuffin band of brothers. He opened his life to them. He spent most of his ministry traveling with them from town to town, and along the way, invested in them the curriculum for kingdom living. The disciples were exposed to Jesus in a way that the massive crowds never experienced.

And of course, the ultimate image of covenant friendship is displayed on the cross. In this act of self-sacrifice, Jesus demonstrated with the most eloquent articulation what it means to love. Through his death, he made a way for God's enemies to share in his friendship. Having blatantly broken our first covenant with him, God invites us into the new covenant through the broken body and poured out blood of Jesus. In this, Miroslav Volf says, God "makes space for the other within the self."[3] It is an act of opening himself wide and inviting the other to become a part of his life. On the cross, God not only opened himself, but he also emptied himself. This is the most shocking, stirring, and irresistible invitation into friendship ever expressed.

the model of the early church

The disciples were marked by their friendship with the Savior. It is no surprise, then, that friendship emerged as one of the distinctive characteristics of the early church. Embedded in this young faith was a rare strand of mutual and selfless love. Rooted in Christ, this love was cultivated within the community and branched out to touch every corner of their context, capturing the imagination of even the strongest critic.

Filled with the Holy Spirit and empowered by the transforming love of Christ, the church broke into existence in Acts 2. It was a dynamic movement marked by prayer, power, and a peculiar kind of love for one another. Verse 42 of the chapter says that the earliest expression of the church of Jesus was known for the way its people cared for and devoted themselves to one another. We are inspired and challenged by this example, and recognize authentic community and covenant friendship as an essential part of every pure and genuine expression of God's church in every context and culture.

how should we practice covenant friendship?

confession

One way to engage in covenant friendship is to practice the discipline of truth telling. When we commit to creating a culture of honesty within our community, we voluntarily make ourselves vulnerable to our friends. Embracing the difficult path of submission and surrender, we trust that our fellow travelers will respond with love to both our confession and confrontation of sin.

Everyone understands that deception undercuts the development of true community. Confession, on the other hand, makes way for it. These twin graces of confession and community overlap and build on one another.

The ancient act of confessing sin, in whatever form, is humbling. But sharing such a personal and private parts of our lives with friends undergirds that relationship with an uncommon kind of trust. It invites those friends into our journey. It asks them to share a burden we were not meant to carry alone. And it introduces the potential for accountability and realized forgiveness.

Confession protects us from ourselves, consistently dismantling the false image we try to construct for the world to see. If the false image is allowed to stand, untested and unexposed, then we slowly become more and more isolated. We retreat deeper into our (fake) selves, distancing our hearts from real friendship—which is to say that we move closer to death. In *Life Together*, Dietrich Bonhoeffer challenges us, "In confession the break-through to community takes place. Sin demands to have a man by himself. It withdraws him from the community. . . . Sin wants to remain unknown. It shuns the light. In the darkness of the unexpressed it poisons the whole being of a person. . . . In confession the light of the Gospel breaks into the darkness and seclusion of the heart."[4]

If we are honest, we will admit that confession frightens us. Our fear might be that if our friends know the truth about us, they will cease to love us. But in this, we tragically misjudge the character of love—the stout, stubborn, unmoving character of the kind of love that serves as the constitution holding covenant friendship in place. Do not trade in this robust love for the weak and neutered idea of acceptance and approval. Love runs deeper and truer.

Love does not dismiss sin. It risks something far more courageous. It risks forgiveness, which looks sin in the eye and calls it by name. Love reminds us of the reality of redemption, proclaiming with a borrowed confidence, "In the name of Jesus Christ, you are forgiven." It bears the weight of guilt with you, and proves through its actions that healing is possible.

radical hospitality

Christian community is crucial to our journey together. It is the sign that we are indeed disciples of Jesus. But the life and teaching of Jesus, even the whole trajectory of the Scriptures, call us to let that love swell up and spill over to those who are seen as being on the outside. We have to zealously guard

143

against the temptation to turn our focus inward, cultivating the community at the expense of loving our neighbor.

The natural desire to be on the inside has the destructive side effect of creating an outside. But this is exactly the kind of status quo construct Jesus disrupted with his revolutionary vision of the world. When he stepped into the story, the old order of things was turned on its head. Love is the great reversal, creating a new reality where suddenly the outsiders are the insiders and the forgotten are the first thought.

This kind of culture should throb and pulse in the souls of Christians and the church. Like the first believers and Jesus himself, we should be known for our radical hospitality toward those on the outside. "Welcome" should be inscribed over our hearts. Our communities of faith should be the one spot on earth where the poor have a place and the homeless feel at home. This kind of open welcome is not a threat to the depth of your already existing friendships. There is no scarcity in love. It has a viral kind of quality that spreads and multiplies and compounds. Let our churches be known for this! Let our churches be criticized and questioned for the kinds of people that call them home! Let the boundaries that mark the inside spread as far and wide as the reach of that blood that makes an inside possible.

now what?

To assist you in the formational practice of covenant friendship, we suggest several steps for you to explore as an individual and in the context of a larger group.

examine

Make a list of those with whom you have relationships. Write not only the expected but all of those with whom you are connected; include coworkers, church people, school friends, acquaintances, and neighbors.

Now take some time to reflect on your friendships. Write the names of those whom you would consider to be most important in your life. What type of people do you usually like to be around? What does this list tell you about what you want or expect out of your friendships?

What are you longing for? Do you long for strong and close friendships? Trust, commonality, accountability, sharing life together?

How do you live out God's reality found in the goodness of truth telling?

In what environments do you tend to exaggerate or bend the truth in order to get what you want or to make yourself seem bigger? Do you find yourself frequenting places, watching news commentators, or reading stories where spin and clever dialogue is revered?

engage

We learned that communitas is a level of relationship that a group experiences when its members pass through some sort of trial together; some call this trial a shared ordeal. Go on a trip where each person in the group has to make critical decisions. Go on a hike, rebuild a car, or remodel a kitchen. Whatever the shared ordeal is, commit to it and see your relationship deepen through the rich chaos.

intentionally schedule time with a close friend. If geographically you are at a distance, then schedule a time to call each other or connect somehow. It is important that you cultivate a time together in order to build trust, support, and encouragement.

form an accountability group. Gather a few friends who will stretch and challenge you.

welcome others. Even when it isn't convenient, welcome others to your home or to a church or social function.

try to listen instead of speak. Don't exaggerate your words and stories. Refuse to spin events and experiences in order to advance yourself.

include family, friends, and the "least of these"— strangers, oppressed, outcasts of your society (perhaps alienated teens, the elderly, refugees, the homeless).

be aware. There are people who are looking for friendship. Be mindful that our desire to be on the inside often has the side effect of creating an outside.

confess to each other. Allow the truth to set you free and your covenant group to surround you with love, grace, and healing. Remember that confession is not just an act, but a deep spirit of openness and transparency, a forsaking of our personal kingdom and abandoning ourselves to God. However, part of learning how to confess is learning how to receive it as well. The depth of one's friendship is not measured by time, space, or commonality, but by the level of authenticity.

Though structured and organized times of confession are important and needed in any covenant group, you will find that organizing events, like a cookout, playing ball, or a movie night is just as important. These spontaneous, everyday occurrences where you can live intentionally amongst each other will shape your character, habits, and way of life. You'll be surprised how fast the way you think, speak, and act will change.

study guide

1. Have you ever experienced or been a part of a covenant friendship? Why or why not?

2. In our culture, rugged individualism is a cardinal virtue. But individualism stands in opposition to the idea of true community because it values the self as first. Have you been a part of a community of people (in your workplace, school, church, or family) that has been frayed or torn apart by individualism? Explain.

3. Think about those you have a relationship with. In what ways have you brought division rather than unity, selfishness rather than selflessness, hostility rather than friendliness, deception rather than truth? Share and discuss.

4. Communitas is a level of relationship that a group experiences when its members pass through some sort of trial together. Why is it difficult for people to go beyond just fellowshiping into a deeper life of communitas? Discuss. Could it be that this epic quest might seem dangerous, messy, and costly? What have been your reasons for experiencing communitas or not? When you have experienced it? What has been the reward? Share.

5. In John 13, Jesus told us that love for others should begin within the body of believers. Does this seem counterintuitive? Shouldn't we love those in the world first rather than ourselves? Why does Jesus tell us to love this way? Discuss.

6. The early church was known for the way its people cared for and devoted themselves to one another (Acts 2:42). What is the church known for today? If you were to interview your friends and people in your workplace, school, and community, how might they answer this question? Try it. Ask a few people you know what the church is known for today. Record your answers and discuss.

7. To truly experience a covenant friendship, confession and truth telling must be at its core. As deception undercuts the development of a true friendship, confession invites the friend into your journey, and asks him or her to share a burden you were not meant to carry alone. This creates opportunity for accountability, realized forgiveness, and redemption. What burdens, lies, fears, and vices are you holding deep inside your soul? Who are the people in your life you can free your soul to through confession and truth telling? Make a list of the people you would like to invite into your journey and seek them out.

8. Like the first believers of the Christian church, we are to be known for our radical hospitality toward those on the outside. This welcome should be inscribed over our hearts and churches. Faith communities should be the place on earth where all people, no matter their race, social status, economic status, or sexual preference should be and feel welcomed and loved, just as Christ welcomes and loves us. Does your church practice welcome and hospitality? What about you?

149

Does your life reflect a theology and belief of welcome and hospitality? Examine and discuss.

9. What ways do you practice and live out covenant friendship? Share your practices and ideas or discover what others are doing at www.facebook.com/awakening grace.

9

generosity

Billionaires Bill Gates, Warren Buffett, and Mark Zuckerburg use their abundant resources for the sake of others. Each have signed an astonishing pledge to give away at least half of their wealth in their lifetimes.[1]

A national megamarket chain gives away 5 percent of its profits to local communities. This works out to about three million dollars a week.[2] This is refreshing news in a corporate culture that worships money and serves the bottom line.

An elderly couple won a multimillion dollar lottery, and instead of splurging the prize on a lavish lifestyle, they gave it away to churches and charities.[3]

These are incredible images of generosity. Out of overflowing wealth and blessing, these people give outside of themselves. How many times have we daydreamed of that opportunity? If only we had more, we would be able to give and accomplish so much more through generosity. With wealth, we could live radically generous lifestyles. Maybe you have already earmarked your imaginary fortune for certain causes and projects that move you. When the windfall comes, you will be ready. You are a philanthropist waiting to happen.

what is generosity?

But Jesus painted a different picture of what generosity looks like. Consider the story of the widow's offering in Luke 21:1–4: "As he looked up, Jesus saw the rich putting their gifts into the temple treasury. He also saw a poor widow put in two very small copper coins. 'I tell you the truth,' he said, 'this poor widow has put in more than all the others. All these people gave their gifts out of their wealth; but she out of her poverty put in all she had to live on.'"

One version captures Jesus' assessment this way: "All these others made offerings that they'll never miss; she gave extravagantly what she couldn't afford—she gave her all!" (v. 4 MSG).

And just like that, Jesus redefined our understanding of generosity. He moved the discussion away from the question of quantity and made the real issue the heart behind the gift. Stunning endowments and trusts don't outrank the sacrifice of a meager offering. In this backwards economy of the kingdom, heart and motive are the ruling currency. The worth of the widow's gifts was the equivalent of a few pennies. Yet we are still talking about her. We might not bother to bend over and pick that up off the sidewalk. But God stopped everything to revel in it. Jesus honored this woman because "she gave extravagantly what she couldn't afford—she gave her all!"

To be clear, this is not to belittle the gracious gifts of the rich; some defy the grip of money by letting it go. Instead, this is intended to magnify the opportunity we have to be generous now with what we have.

the new standard

This act of redefining our understanding of an issue was common practice for Jesus all through the Gospels. He consistently set a new standard for what it means to live in and live out the reality of God's kingdom. He proclaimed the end of legalism's reign and introduced a new freedom won by grace and love. In light of this pattern, people often draw the conclusion that, in this new covenant, the Old Testament principle of tithing (giving a tenth of all you earn to God as an offering) is obsolete.

But the new covenant doesn't destroy the old. It completes it. In fact, we repeatedly see Jesus raise the bar on expectations to shocking new heights. (Think: "You have heard it said, 'love your neighbor.' But I tell you 'love your enemies.'") He did the same again here. The Old Testament standard was to give 10 percent. You can make the case that the New Testament standard is to give all you have and all you are. Again, Jesus breaks us free from the tyranny of legalism but binds us to the highest law—love. In this, we find our fullest freedom.

153

Jesus called for more than walking the line on a rule or regulation. Jesus invited us into the joy of generous living: the daring, frightening, courageous act of giving ourselves away. This is the new standard—the new normal—marked by trust-filled, full-hearted generosity.

the church and the money problem

Before we go any further, let's be honest about something. The unfortunate truth is that the moment we start talking about money in conjunction with Christianity, things can get pretty uncomfortable; and for good reason. Tragically, some have manipulated hearts and minds in order to open up purses and pockets. And now, because of some of God's representatives, the church as a whole is often painted with the same sad stain.

But God is not a thief. And God is not greedy. In fact, Scripture reveals a God whose sharpest anger is reserved for two crimes: idolatry and the exploitation of the poor by the powerful, especially in the name of religion. It is this divine frame of heart that sparked the righteous rage of Jesus in the temple (Matt. 21:12–13; Mark 11:15–17; Luke 19:45–46; John 2:13–16). Since the poor generally did not have their own livestock to bring for sacrifice, they had to purchase animals from merchants at the temple. Realizing they were dealing with necessary commodities, these merchants would often run up the price. The laws of supply and demand had smiled favorably on them, and they were taking full advantage of the situation. This turned worship into a profit machine and an unfair burden for the poor.

Enter Jesus. Suddenly, tables started flying, animals scattered, and crooks dove for cover. This is a sign of how God feels about manipulating money in his name. He will not take it.

why practice generosity?

We acknowledge that money can be a sensitive, sometimes painful subject to talk about in connection with Jesus. So then, why do it? Why don't we just skip past and skirt around the issue to avoid the awkward conversation? Surely this book would have been fine without this chapter, right? Actually, no. It would not be complete without addressing the vital practice of how we interact with our money and the correlating spiritual ramifications. And judging from how much attention Jesus gave to the topic, he seems to agree.

why does Jesus want my money?

Jesus talked about money repeatedly throughout the Gospels. But it's not because he wants your money. It's because he wants you. And he understands that the two are intimately intertwined.

In the Sermon on the Mount, Jesus stated plainly, "Where your treasure is, there your heart will be also" (Matt. 6:21). He understood that we reach for what we love, and love what we reach for. We hide the things we love in our hearts, and give our hearts away to them. As E. Stanley Jones said, "Whatever has your attention has you."[4]

155

Jesus wants us to reach for him, to hide him in our hearts, and to give our hearts away to him alone. He knows that money makes a weak yet tyrannical god, and its promises of happiness and security are bankrupt. He's watched far too many rich young rulers choose that empty hope for fear of empty hands.

It's not that Jesus wants to steal our money; he is out to steal our hearts. And that is why he warns of the crucial role that money plays in our discipleship journey. The purpose is not to fill the baskets. The purpose is to fashion a generous community and shape generous hearts.

the blueprint

The early church is our model for practicing generosity. Acts 2 tells the story of this grassroots movement, sparked by the death, resurrection, and ascension of Jesus and the outpouring of the Holy Spirit at Pentecost. These believers were radically transformed by the fullness of salvation, and every part of their lives came under the unrivaled reign of God. To look at them is to see holiness alive and in motion.

This distilled, pure strand of sanctification pulsing in them stirred an unswerving courage, unbreakable unity, and uncommon generosity—all of which produced waves of awe through the community around them, and for good reason. Acts 2:45 records what generosity looked like for them: "Selling their possessions and goods, they gave to anyone as he had need." This strange sacrifice reflected the character of their Savior and captured the imagination of their culture.

how should we practice generosity?

promiscuous generosity

The first generations of Christians became identifiable by the peculiar way they gave themselves away. It was both inspiring and perplexing to outside observers. The reports and rumors made their way through the Roman Empire and all the way to the emperor himself.

History tells us that Emperor Julian marveled over the shocking behavior of these believers. He remarked, "Their success lies in charity to strangers . . . The impious Galileans [because they did not worship Rome's gods] support both their own poor and ours as well."[5]

The empire brought oppression. The kingdom unleashed generosity.

Another ancient writer commented on the countercultural identity and influence of Christians in the empire. He observed that, in stark contrast to the environment in which they lived, the followers of Jesus would not share their beds, but they freely shared their table. This led Tim Keller to conclude, "They were promiscuous with their monies, not their bodies."[6]

Promiscuous generosity—what a stunning thought. This curious kind of charity proclaimed a potent critique of the system and a poignant image of God's kingdom. With purity in their lives and love in their

157

hearts, these first Christians were signs and symbols of the new normal inaugurated by Jesus.

managing our money

Now understand that when we speak of promiscuous generosity, we are not advocating financial irresponsibility. This is not an attack on sound principles of stewardship. It is our responsibility to manage our money. But we must be careful or our money will manage us.

There is a danger for us to use the concept of stewardship as a protection against the risk and danger of giving ourselves away. But remember what stewardship means. It is not the cautious guarding of our finances; it is the understanding that what we have does not belong to us. It is not the act of burying our resources safely away from the risk of waste and loss; it is the recognition that all we have has been entrusted to us by God. And he requires us to earn, save, spend, and give those resources with that as the governing principle.

We can easily hide behind the front of stewardship in order to hold onto more of our possessions. But that is not stewardship; it is idolatry disguised as stewardship. Idolatry is more than happy to be mistaken for something else. That, in fact, is all idolatry is. It lives by that mistake.

simplicity

158

One way to guard against the creeping idolatry of money is to intentionally embrace a lifestyle of simplicity. To live simply is to be keenly aware of how we make use of our resources. It is one way to purposefully carve out space for generosity in our lives.

In the spirit of the Acts 2 blueprint, simplicity is a subversive move, a countercultural response to a society consumed by consumerism. It doesn't indulge every impulse to buy the next thing that captures our fleeting attention and affection. Instead, it cultivates a thoughtful examination of those impulses. It assesses the impact (positive and negative) of our purchases on us and others.

To live simply is to resist the grip of cluttered accumulation and recognize that we are sustained by the grace and goodness of God. This style of life centers on a gratitude for what God provides. The unnecessary gets stripped away. Our possessions become gifts from God and not trophies of our earning power.

Simplicity is not asceticism, a self-inflicted punishment to beat materialism into submission. Instead, it is a healthy expression of our freedom in and dependence on the triune God. It is a Sabbath rest from the frantic race to keep up with our consumer culture. It declares that what we own will not own us. Simplicity acknowledges that the only sustainable way to live is in surrendered trust. And by practicing this surrender, we open up room for greater generosity. By spending less on things we don't need, we find the margin to give more for those in need.

put your money where your mission is

We are called to model generosity as individuals, intentionally leveraging our personal resources for the sake of God and others. We are challenged to embody the same self-sacrifice as communities as well. Our churches ask for generosity from our people. But churches should, in turn, lead the way in demonstrating a collective kind of promiscuous generosity. Our friends at Ekklesia Church in Raleigh, North Carolina, are doing this in a compelling way. The people in this church plant decided from the very beginning that they wanted to give themselves away. Inspired by the blueprint of Acts 2 and the abundant generosity of God, they have covenanted to give away one-third of everything given to Ekklesia. They send this money outside of their walls, into their community, and around the world.

In less than a year of meeting for worship, they've helped neighbors with heat bills in winter, provided food for the local rescue mission, and even treated their homeless friends to outings of burgers, bowling, and baseball games. They have supported the Love Your Neighbor House in Indianapolis, Indiana, and an after-school program on the southside of Chicago. And in Moneni, Swaziland, Ekklesia fully funds a care point that feeds, educates, and provides medical care for 215 children. They are an inspiring new chapter in an ancient story. Moved by the self-emptying love of God, they are responding by giving themselves away as well.

now what?

To assist you in the formational practice of generosity, we suggest several steps for you to explore as an individual and in the context of a larger group.

examine

The opposite of indulgence is frugality, which refrains from the desire of wanting more, and even the appearance of wanting more.

Now wrestle honestly with this question: What (or who) motivates your generosity? Do you want to be generous, or do you simply want to be known as generous? Gary Thomas shares that "material generosity is just the start of inner freedom. There is a spiritual generosity as well, a disposition that leads us to give and serve rather than crave to receive."[7] If people were asked to evaluate your life based on how you spend money and your actions toward those around you, would they say you are one who gives and serves, or craves and receives?

follow

The practice of generosity trains us to be comfortable without stimulation and gratification of our desires (see Prov. 21:17; 23:4; 25:8; 1 Tim. 5:5–6; 6:7–11, 17–19). These passages and Jesus' teachings tell us that our hearts and treasures are intimately intertwined.

Track your finances over the next week or the next month. Where is your money going? Does this match

161

up with your heart? What did you learn about the connection between the two?

Read the passages above, along with this passage in Matthew 10:8: "Heal the sick, raise the dead, cleanse those who have leprosy, drive out demons. Freely you have received, freely give." These passages reflect the nature of one's character, for out of our character flows action. Does your life reflect the generosity of Christ? Is your character a reflection of his?

risk

Giving ourselves away is never easy. But Jesus invites us to live in the raised standard where courageous, trust-filled generosity becomes the new normal. What would your life look like if you gave yourself away?

Walk around your neighborhood or school, or think about your work environment and dream of what it would look like if the Spirit of God transformed it. How would those places look different? How would the actions of people there begin to look different? Give yourself to these environments, these places in which you have influence, and allow God to move through you. What you are dreaming can become reality. Move, take the risk, and join God in his transformational work!

study guide

1. Jesus redefines our understanding of generosity. He moves the discussion away from the question of quantity and makes the real issue the heart behind the gift. Have you ever been the receiver of a gift that was not extravagant or expensive, but because it was given from a creative, thoughtful, and genuine heart it gave you great joy? Explain.

2. Jesus calls for more than walking the line on a rule or regulation. Jesus invites us into the joy of generous living: the daring, frightening, courageous act of giving ourselves away. This is the new standard— the new normal—marked by trust-filled, full-hearted generosity. Do you find it difficult to live a generous life such as this? What exactly does the act of giving yourself away look like to you? Discuss.

3. Some Christian leaders and ministries manipulate the hearts and minds of people to get them to open their purses and pockets so they can move forward their agenda instead of God's. Because of this, the overall church is often painted with the same sad stain. Do you think the world has a good or poor view of the church and money? What about their view of Christians and money? Ask a few friends or family members what they think. How do you personally see it?

4. Jesus talks about the issue of money repeatedly throughout the Gospels, showing that our money (or possessions) and lives are intimately intertwined. Do

you agree that our finances, possessions, and money are closely connected to who we are as people?

5. Generosity is part of the fullness of salvation. Have you ever thought about the outflow of a generous heart being so closely connected to one's salvation? Have you seen generosity as an outward sign of your heart, will, and commitment to Christ? Why is generosity a good measurement of one's transformation and commitment to Christ?

6. One byproduct of generosity is the commitment to live and think simply. However, simplicity is not asceticism, a self-inflicted punishment to beat materialism into submission. Rather, it is a healthy expression of freedom in and dependence on the triune God. Is living out a life of simplicity even possible in today's complex and material world? What makes living out simplicity unusual by today's standards? Discuss.

7. How can you put your money where your mission is? First, ask yourself, what is your mission? What is God doing around you, and how can you give and participate with him? How will you live a life of generosity? Pray. Give. Act.

10
creative expression

We recently came across a funny image that caught us by surprise. It comes from a blog called "Indexed" by Jessica Hagy. Jessica posts witty observations in the form of simple, hand-drawn infographics on index cards. Below is her highly scientific pie chart on creativity.[1]

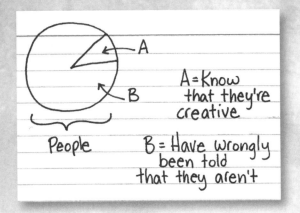

With quirky humor and simplicity, she cuts to the core of an important issue: Most of us don't see ourselves as creative. We've been wrongly told or have passively believed that we are not.

what is creative expression?

imago dei

Our entire story of humanity began with an act of creativity. Not only did God create the cosmos, he created us—in his image. This is the first and deepest truth about us. Out of divine love, we were created in the image of a creative God.

Out of this foundation grows countless implications for our theology and practice. It sets the trajectory for how we understand God's love, salvation, the doctrine of sin, and our relationship to creation and each other.

But it also affirms a truth too often lost—we are all creative. Within every one of us is the spark of creativity that we inherited from God. Unfortunately, most don't believe it.

Somewhere along the way, we grow up and grow out of our imaginations—probably about the same time that our crayon creations start getting graded. We start to get sorted into different categories based on our areas of academic excellence (or seeming lack thereof). We realize that some people are naturally gifted artists or musicians and that our brains don't function in that same way. We label those friends as "creative" and surmise that we are not.

But our theology tells us something radically different. Our point here is not that every person should try to be a musician or painter. Everyone is gifted and needs to discover and unleash those gifts for the glory of God. We find it ironic that most have a limited idea of what creativity can mean. We need a broad definition of creativity and a bold invitation to express it. You are unique and uniquely gifted. And how you express your passions and gifts can be an act of worship.

St. Francis of Assisi helps us toward expanding our understanding of creativity. He said, "He who works with his hands and his head and his heart is an artist."[2] Aristotle is also helpful here, adding, "Art is our capacity to make."[3] But perhaps artist Makoto Fujimara hits closest to what we mean. He says, "Art expresses who we are."[4]

When we express our creativity, we express who we are, and in a sense, who God is. While we are not trying to change how art is defined and recognized, we do embrace the way these thoughts open up the borders and boundaries of creativity. We affirm that when we engage our diverse passions and gifts in the acts of making and creating we are reflecting the divine nature.

why should we practice creative expression?

exposing God's genius

God creates each of us uniquely, with specific gifts and passions. When we discover and unleash these gifts and passions we point to the one who gives them and delights in our design. In this act of expression, we expose God's genius. What does creativity look like for you? What loves and joys and dreams has God written on your soul?

Are you an artist, musician, writer, or poet? Perhaps you are gifted in math, science, technology, or medicine. Maybe you love building things with your hands, tending a garden, cultivating a farm, cooking food, or repairing cars. Do you have a passion for filmmaking? Theater? Design? Storytelling? Maybe you are skilled at solving problems, crafting strategies, building systems, shepherding projects, or leading teams.

Teachers. Photographers. Nurses. Composers. Pastors. Architects. Engineers. Leaders. Activists. Entrepreneurs. Journalists. Inventors. Social Workers. God invites all of us to express who we are through the limitless ways in which he has designed us. And when you come alive to who you are and how you are gifted, you become a walking witness of his genius.

what if . . . ?

People respond to different forms of communication. And it is crucial to realize that we have been gifted to tell the story in a way that is unique to us and yet will resonate with other hearts and souls. There are people just like us who come alive when they are building or repairing something with their hands. What if you organized a community building project to benefit elderly widows by repairing homes for people who can't do it for themselves? What kind of message of God's grace and love would that communicate? Or what if your friends decide to change the oil and service the cars for single moms in your neighborhood? How would that open up the reality of God's love in the eyes of those moms?

What if you write a play or a song? What if you teach photography or piano to inner-city kids? What if you deliver your prized, secret family recipe dish to the homeless man at the corner or to the police station or fire department? You can write notes of encouragement to the teachers at the local school or start a nonprofit organization. Or a clothing line. Or a studio.

What if you give time at the local nursing home or after-school program? What if you make it a point to remember the forgotten? What if you hand out flowers downtown? Or create a mural for your city? Or revive a park? Or . . .

What if you discover what you love, and set that love loose on the world? What if you discover your gift and turn around and give it away?

This is not just about doing good in a quasi-spiritual, morally nebulous sort of way. This is about expressing who you are. This is about creatively expressing and unleashing God's mercy through the common acts of your life.

the new stained glass

In the earlier chapter on worship, we mentioned that the breathtaking works of stained glass that grace the windows of our churches and cathedrals actually serve as a way of communicating the salvation story to worshipers. As the sun shines through them, intricate images of grace and mercy come alive in the glass. So what will become our new stained glass? What art forms will emerge as a way of telling the story in creative ways? Film? Poetry? Design? Music? Architecture?

the transcending power of beauty

Art and beauty have a disarming quality that allows the walls to come down. Simultaneously, beauty draws us in. It is compelling. It invites our participation and our interpretation of the truth that lives within it. Art and beauty are stunning avenues through which we are challenged to respond to what we see.

Art critiques us, although we often think of it the other way around. Beauty has a way of cutting through our defenses. It disrupts. It unsettles. In the process and in that unexpected space of dissonance, it communicates to us in a manner that words often cannot. In fact, beauty forces us to come up with words and language to articulate what we experience.

Sometimes, on those rare and most welcome of occasions, no words can be found. Or the ones we can find simply will not do. In those moments, beauty itself is the language. Perhaps this is why people have referred to beauty as transcendent. It is one of the qualities that is honored and cherished across cultural barriers. It's as if we do not need to be taught to appreciate beauty. The love of it is innate. It has the strength to rise above and barrel through the boundaries and borders that separate people.

This transcendent power of beauty is captured in a scene from the stirring film *The Shawshank Redemption* The movie follows the fading lives of several prison inmates, serving sentences within Shawshank's unforgiving walls. In an act of costly courage, one inmate named Andy Dufresne manages to briefly broadcast Mozart's "Canzonetta sull'aria" from *The Marriage of Figaro* over the prison's loudspeakers. As the music pours out over the prison yard, brilliant cinematography captures a massive crowd of hardened men stunned and shocked by the surprising beauty of the frozen moment.

A fellow inmate named Red recounts the experience in these words: "I have no idea to this day what those two Italian ladies were singing about. Truth is, I don't wanna know. Some things are best left unsaid. I like to think they were singing about something so beautiful it can't be expressed in words, and makes your heart ache because of it. I tell you, those voices soared higher and farther than anybody in a gray place dares to dream. It was like some beautiful bird flapped into our drab little cage and made those walls dissolve away, and for the briefest of moments, every last man at Shawshank felt free."[5]

That is the power of beauty. It breaks through darkness and smuggles hope into unexpected places. Beauty, in a word, transcends.

how should we practice creative expression?

integrating imagination

Have you noticed how many questions are being posed in this chapter? While most of the chapters in this book set out to explore answers concerning the practice at hand, some paragraphs in this chapter consist solely of questions. Why?

This approach is intentional because when it comes to the idea of creative expression as a spiritual practice, the potential is limitless. There are possibilities and innovations that we have yet to dream of. Our hope is not to define what this looks like for you, but to spark a sort of mental momentum. We want to open your eyes to this truth, and stand back as the Holy Spirit works out the implications in your life. Our prayer is that God awakens your imagination and you begin to integrate it into your spiritual journey and expression of your love for him.

calling all creatives!

Churches, commission your artists. We all have people sitting in our services who are humming with potential and creativity. Let's learn how to unleash their gifts for God's glory. One word of warning: shepherd, but don't try to control. Be free with your permission and blessing. Empower. Risk the chaos that is often found right at the edge of creativity. Let your people stretch you beyond your point of comfort. Celebrate the diversity of skills and joys within your family. And this expression does not have to happen within the framework of a Sunday worship setting. Unleash the creativity of your people into the community. Ask them how you can love your town through their gifts. Have you ever considered the potential of art as mission or of creativity as proclamation? What could that look like in your setting?

Artists, consider this your commission. You have been given a unique gift. And the world needs what you have. Tell the story of redemption. Create. Build. Experiment. Dream. Risk. Grow. If the Holy Spirit has sparked an idea, given a burden, or stirred a passion, then that is all the permission you need to go and do it. A word of warning for you as well: don't expect somebody else to do this for you. God gave this passion to you, not everyone else. So don't be upset if your friends or your church are slow to get on board. Start small. Be patient. And one more thing to remember: The gift is yours, but the glory isn't. Your gift is not about you. It is always about the one who gave it in the first place. Let your life boldly point back to God. Use your life to tell his story. And tell it well.

from imitation to innovation

As churches, we need to embrace this practice of creative expression as well. We need to discover new ways of expressing God's genius instead of chasing after trends and copying the success of others. Live your own story. Look around. Where are the opportunities to express who you are? How can you tell the story of redemption in a compelling way in your community?

God has more dreams for you than your head can handle. He who has faithfully loved your neighbors through you is only getting started. He who transforms lives through your ministry is leading you into new frontiers for his glory.

So don't imitate. Innovate. Be inspired and stretched by the stories of others—not threatened or jealous. Creativity is not competitive but collaborative. Learn from the faithfulness of others while asking what faithfulness looks like for you.

remember who you are

One last thing: Remember who you are. Remember where you came from. Again, our entire story of humanity began with an act of creativity. Not only did God create the cosmos, he created us—in his image.

This is the first and deepest truth about us. Out of divine love, we are created in the image of a creative God. His life pulses in us. His delight pours over us. He is crazy about you, and he can't wait to see what you might do together with him. Don't look at what you don't have and doubt. Look at what you have been given and believe.

now what?

To assist you in the formational practice of creative expression, we suggest several steps for you to explore as an individual and in the context of a larger group.

discover

In pinpointing your passions and discovering what you love, take some time to engage the following questions.

discover your passions.

1. If you could do anything in the world, what would you do?
2. What is your deepest hope and wildest dream?
3. What jobs would you do for free?
4. What classes do you look forward to most?
5. What kind of stories, movies, and books draw you in?
6. How do you spend your free time?
7. What do you look forward to? Make time for?

175

Also helpful: What upsets you? What angers you? What drains you?

discover your gifts. Consider the following questions to discover where you are most naturally gifted.

1. What are you good at? On a scale of one to ten, where are you a ten?
2. What do you receive the most compliments for?
3. What kind of work or activity energizes you?
4. What kind of work doesn't feel like work?
5. When do people seek you out for help?
6. When do you feel in the zone? What is your "sweet spot"?

Also helpful: What are you just flat out terrible at? What kinds of activities or work do you dread? What kinds of work drain you?

discover where your passions and gifts converge.

1. Where do you notice patterns of convergence?
2. Where do your gifts and passions seem to overlap?
3. What intriguing combinations do you see beginning to emerge?
4. What does this say about how God has created you?
5. How can you express who you are through worship to God for the sake of the world?

examine

Read Genesis 1. Read through it slowly. Breathe in the creative words that God used to speak nothing into existence.

Remember your days as a young child? Making up games that seem to have no ending, drawing pictures that never looked liked those Disney characters, or acting out a character from your favorite movie or book with no hopes of receiving an Oscar. What were some of your favorite creative moments as a child? Were you good at drawing, singing, acting, dancing, or playing games?

Do you remember those days? What happened to them? When did these innate, creative urgencies quit existing? Do you remember when you transitioned out of this imaginative and creative period of your life? Somewhere along the way, we have evaluated, graded, identified, and categorized ourselves as either an artist or not. As John Stott stated, "It is my conviction that our heavenly Father says the same to us every day: 'My dear child, you must always remember who you are.'"[6] Have we forgotten who we really are?

Do you believe that our worship is an expression of our creative beings? What does worship look like in your life? In your church?

In your life, church, and community, where do you see the expression of creativity? Now examine the movie, music, and art industries in your area. Through these places of expression, what do you think influences these folks to be so creative? Who or what are they worshiping? Do you see God being worshiped in these places? If God is being worshiped creatively outside of the church, is it possible that God can be creatively worshiped within the church? Does location limit one's creative expression and worship of God?

reflect

Imagine for a moment the majestic creation of God. Form a picture in your mind of the most beautiful scene in creation. Now draw that image. What do you see? Mountains? Forests? The ocean? People? The nations? Do you know what God sees when he thinks of the most beautiful scene in creation? You! You are his greatest work. You have been created in his own image, and he looked at you and said that you are "very good," the best of the best!

Do you truly believe that you are "very good"; that God Almighty truly believes in you and loves you? Dwell on these truths for a few minutes and let them soak into your heart and soul.

Now read Psalm 139:13–16.

In verse 14 we see the word *praise*. When was the last time you praised God for how you are made? Try doing something that is out of the ordinary in thanking God for his love and desire for you.

In verse 16, we read how all the days are ordained, thus there is an intimate involvement of God in our past, present, and future. Even the most painful events of your past have been redeemed by him and used for your formation and his glory!

engage

Write a letter or song, paint on a canvas, or create a space that will be sacred, expressing your love and appreciation for God and all he has done for you.

Find some time to use your hands and plant some herbs or vegetables. If you are in the city, maybe invite your neighbors and create a community garden. Cultivate the ground, get your hands dirty, and nurture the plants to full growth. After giving care and attention, when it is time for bloom or harvest, give praise and thanks to God for his creative order and the blessing of life.

Write a worship song for your congregation. You know your community and how God is moving in and through it. Reflect on this movement through words and music and allow his symphony, the church, to sing it aloud!

study guide

1. The entire story of humanity began with an act of creativity. Your expression of your unique gifts can be an act of worship. Referring back to Genesis 1 and Psalm 139, have you ever thought of the creation story as a story of creativity, of careful precision knitted by the hand of God? Discuss these passages. What questions do you have about God's creativity through the lens of the creation story?

2. What are your thoughts about the concept that how you express your passions and gifts is part of your worship to God? Do you agree or disagree? Why?

3. We read three statements from three great thinkers on how our creativity is a part of who we are as created beings: St. Francis of Assisi, Aristotle, and Mokoto Fujimara. Which of the three statements do you resonate with? Why are the arts such a great influence on the minds and hearts of people? Discuss.

4. No matter what your interests and passions or where your career path takes you, God invites you to express who you are in the unique way in which he has designed you. Have you ever thought that God favors more those who are in full-time ministry or those who have committed to serve God overseas or in the inner city as a missionary? God has called all of us to creatively express ourselves through what we do, glorifying him. No matter if

you are an engineer, stockbroker, student, nurse, pastor, inventor, activist, or graphic designer, God has called you to be a walking witness of his genius! Come up with ten ways you can be a walking witness, a creative expression, today. Share with your group and discuss.

5. Some of the most beautiful art known to man are the works of stained glass that grace the windows of our churches and cathedrals. However, the question for us today is, "What new forms will emerge as a way of telling the story in creative ways?" Brainstorm ways you, your group, and your church can creatively tell the story. The only limit is your imagination. What did you come up with? Share, discuss, and put into practice.

6. Art and beauty have a disarming quality that allows the walls to come down; beauty draws us in. Do you think the church has lost its influence on the arts, failing to communicate the reality of God and his presence within it? Examine this question, and reflect on what you see in your church and community. What conclusion did you come up with? Explain.

7. Although we often think of it the other way around, art critiques us. Beauty has a way of cutting through our defenses, and sometimes it forces us to come up with words to articulate what we are experiencing. But on those occasions that no words can be found, beauty itself is the language. Beauty

transcends. Can you identify in your life this transcendent beauty? Reflect on this question for a moment, and make a list of what you see. Share.

conclusion

ending with a beginning

The Psalms begin with a beautiful image of what a vibrant life in Christ looks like. And it seems like a fitting way for us to end.

Psalm 1 describes the person in relationship with God "like a tree planted by streams of water, which yields its fruit in season and whose leaf does not wither" (v. 3). As we close this part of the journey, these poetic lines remind us of where we have been together and send us into our next steps with courage and heart.

like a tree planted . . .

The tree doesn't prosper because of its own stress and strength. But rooted in the heart and mind of God, the life on the limbs is nurtured by the fertile soil of grace. And nowhere does the verse promise that the tree will be protected from the elements—it is exposed to the threatening winds and turbulent storms. Yet the deep roots hold this tree in place. What can shake this life?

by streams of water . . .

Throughout the Psalms and the scope of Scripture, the image of water takes on spiritual significance. Rivers and streams are repeatedly used to represent the renewing presence of the Spirit of God. And that is what is happening here. The tree standing on the banks draws its strength from the stream. The fruit we see above ground is the result of what is happening beneath the surface.

which yields its fruit in season . . .

This is an encouraging reminder that life hangs on a rhythm of seasons. In one season, the fruit of growth is out in the open. In another, the signs are not. There will be seasons of light and dark, pain and joy, rapid growth and cold stagnation. When you find yourself in a season when growth isn't coming easily, don't give up. You don't burn down the orchard in winter.

and whose leaf does not wither . . .

Stay rooted in the heart and mind of the Father through these sustaining spiritual practices. Continue to draw strength from the Spirit's cultivating work in these means of grace. You will find that God's awakening grace is always shaping you into the image of Christ for the sake of the world.

notes

Chapter 1

1. J. D. Walt is vice president for Community Life at Asbury Theological Seminary in Wilmore, Kentucky. Read more from J. D. on worship and spiritual practices at www.jdwalt.com.

2. C. S. Lewis, *The Silver Chair*, The Chronicles of Narnia (New York: HarperCollins, 1953), 23.

Chapter 2

1. M. Robert Mulholland, Jr., *Shaped by the Word: The Power of Scripture in Spiritual Formation* (Nashville: Upper Room, 1985), 54–55.

2. Richard Foster, *Celebration of Discipline: The Path to Spiritual Growth* (New York: HarperCollins, 1998), 15.

3. Dietrich Bonhoeffer, *Life Together: A Discussion of Christian Fellowship* (New York: HarperCollins, 1954), 83.

4. Mulholland, 43.

5. For great helps and resources on lectio divina, see the Lectio Divina Bible Study series from Wesleyan Publishing House, www.wphonline.com.

Chapter 3

1. Wendell Berry, *Jayber Crow* (Berkeley, Calif.: CounterPoint, 2000), 54.

2. Richard Foster, *Celebration of Discipline: The Path to Spiritual Growth* (New York: HarperCollins, 1998), 33.

3. Rueben P. Job and Norman Shawchuck, eds., *A Guide to Prayer for Ministers and Other Servants* (Nashville: Upper Room, 1983), 72.

4. Dallas Willard, *The Divine Conspiracy: Rediscovering Our Hidden Life in God* (New York: HarperCollins, 1997), 191.

5. Doug Pagitt, *BodyPrayer: The Posture of Intimacy with God* (Colorado Springs: Waterbrook, 2005), 4–5.

6. Ibid., 5.

Chapter 4

1. Lyrics from "You Never Let Go" by Matt Redman.

2. Richard Foster, *Celebration of Discipline: The Path to Spiritual Growth* (New York: HarperCollins, 1998), 158.

3. Joan Chittister, *The Liturgical Year: The Spiraling Adventure of the Spiritual Life*, The Ancient Practices Series (Nashville: Thomas Nelson, 2009), 48.

4. Foster, 158.

5. Robert E. Webber, *Ancient-Future Time: Forming Spirituality through the Christian Year* (Grand Rapids, Mich.: Baker, 2004), 169.

6. Abraham Joshua Heschel, *God in Search of Man: A Philosophy of Judiasm* (New York: Farrar, Straus and Giroux, 1976), 156–157.

7. C. S. Lewis, *Letters to Malcolm: Chiefly on Prayer* (New York: Harcourt, 1963), 75.

8. Brother Lawrence, *The Practice of the Presence of God* (Grand Rapids, Mich.: Spire Books, 1967), 16.

9. Ibid., 44.

10. Reference given by Dallas Willard (GM720 Spirituality and Ministry, seminar notes, June 2010).

Chapter 5

1. This quote is a frequent favorite of Dr. Cornel West. We first encountered it through the documentary film *Call + Response*. Read more online at http://www.callandresponse.com/about.php and http://rejectapathy.com/loss-of-innocents/features/19511-what-love-looks-like-in-public.

2. Robert Ellsberg, ed., *Flannery O'Connor: Spiritual Writings* (New York: Orbis Books, 2003), 47.

3. E. Stanley Jones, *The Christ of the Indian Road* (New York: Abingdon, 1925), 52.

4. "History of the Salvation Army," accessed November 15, 2011, http://www.salvationarmyusa.org/usn/www_usn_2.nsf/vw-dynamic-arrays/

816DE20E46B88B2685257435005070FA?
openDocument&charset =utf-8.

5. The Bridge Project, accessed November 15, 2011, http://thebridgeproject.weebly.com.

6. Abraham Joshua Heschel, *God in Search of Man: A Philosophy of Judiasm* (New York: Farrar, Straus and Giroux, 1976), 252.

Chapter 6

1. Sandra Richter, *The Epic of Eden: A Christian Entry into the Old Testament* (Downers Grove, Ill.: InterVarsity, 2008), 105.

2. Ibid., 106.

3. Abraham Joshua Heschel, *The Sabbath* (New York: Farrar, Straus and Giroux, 2005).

4. Nancy Sleeth, *Go Green, Save Green: A Simple Guide to Saving Time, Money, and God's Green Earth* (Carol Stream, Ill.: Tyndale, 2009), 195.

5. Ibid.

Chapter 7

1. Francis Schaeffer and Udo Middlemann, *Pollution and the Death of Man* (Wheaton, Ill.: Tyndale, 1970), 69.

2. Ibid., 59.

3. For a great explanation of the relationship between Gnosticism and the Christian response to creation care, read Christopher Bounds, "God's Ongoing Redemption of All Creation" in Joseph Coleson, ed.,

Care of Creation (Indianapolis, Ind.: Wesleyan Publishing House, 2010), 47–59.

4. C. S. Lewis, *Miracles* (New York: Harper-Collins, 1947), 179.

5. Tertullian, *De Testimonio Animae.*

6. St. John of Damascus, *Treatise.*

7. "Creation Care throughout the Ages," *Blessed Earth: Suggestions for Honoring God's Creation,* accessed November 15, 2011, http://www.blessed earth.org/wp-content/uploads/ 2011/09/Creation-Care-Quotes.pdf.

8. Ibid.

Chapter 8

1. C. S. Lewis, *The Four Loves* (New York: Harcourt Brace, 1960), 72.

2. Alan Hirsch, *The Forgotten Ways: Reactivating the Missional Church* (Grand Rapids, Mich.: Brazos, 2006), 218.

3. Miroslav Volf, *Exclusion and Embrace: A Theological Exploration of Identity, Otherness, and Reconciliation* (Nashville: Abingdon, 1996), 154.

4. Dietrich Bonhoeffer, *Life Together: A Discussion of Christian Fellowship* (New York: HarperCollins, 1954), 112.

Chapter 9

1. Lev Grossman, "Person of the Year 2010: Mark Zuckerberg." *TIME,* December 15, 2010,

http://www.time.com/time/specials/packages/article/0, 28804,2036683_2037183_2037185-3,00.html.

2. "Grants," accessed November 15, 2011, http://sites.target.com/site/en/company/page.jsp?content Id=WCMP04-031767.

3. "Couple Wins $11M; Gives Almost All of it Away," CBS News, November 5, 2010, http://www.cbs news.com/stories/2010/11/05/earlyshow/main70 25286.shtml.

4. This quote is widely attributed to E. Stanley Jones, groundbreaking Methodist missionary to India.

5. Timothy Keller, Generous Giving, Inc., *Power, Change, and Money*, accessed November 15, 2011, http://library.generousgiving.org/images/ uploaded/rl_KELLER_Power_ Change_Money.pdf.

6. Ibid.

7. Gary Thomas, *The Glorious Pursuit: Embracing the Virtues of Christ* (Colorado Springs: NavPress, 1998), 110.

Chapter 10

1. Jessica Hagy, "Your Imagination Is Real," *Indexed* (blog), April 4, 2011, http://thisisindexed.com/ category/value/page/2/.

2. Widely attributed to St. Francis of Assisi.

3. Quoted by Makoto Fujimara, *Refractions: A Journey of Faith, Art, and Culture* (Colorado Springs: NavPress, 2009), 110.

4. Ibid.

5. Stephen King and Frank Darabont, *The Shawshank Redemption,* directed by Frank Darabont (Beverly Hills, Calif.: Castle Rock Entertainment, 1994), DVD.

6. John Stott, *Authentic Christianity* (Downers Grove, Ill.: InterVarsity, 1996), 215–216.